Just a girl with anxiety

A Journey to Mental Freedom

Jennifer Bitner

Mind Fitness Trainer + Success Mentor

www.jenniferbitner.com

Just A Girl With Anxiety

A Journey To Mental Freedom

Jennifer Bitner is a global leading educator on emotional aromatherapy, a success mentor, founder of Mind Fitness™, and professional speaker. She spent over a decade of her life determined to break free from the chains of a mental health disorder, which she hid behind the mask of a successful corporate career woman. Now she's here to share her story, perils, and wisdom with the rest of the world, teaching people how to have more freedom and less stress.

I dedicate this book to all the Mind Fitness Warriors out there who know they deserve the greatest life and optimal mental health.

I also want to credit my sister-in-law Lyndee, who spent the last month of her pregnancy editing and arranging the flow of the many blog posts that were compiled to create this book. Love you!

CONTENTS

Introduction

September 5, 2012: I sat at my computer for hours staring at a Facebook status I had just poured my heart into. I wanted to hit the post button so badly but was riddled with fear.

What will people think? Will they judge me? Will they think I'm weak or treat me differently?

For six years I had never been socially open about my journey with mental health: the 24/7 anxiety, multiple panic attacks per day, the chronic stress I was under. I hid as much of it as I could in an effort to appear "normal."

I would lie to my friends about why I wouldn't travel places, why I would leave events early all the time. I did my best to hide this illness because I could.

It was invisible to everyone else.

So why do I believe you need to read this book?
Well, if you have ever suffered from any type of mental block or mental "dis-ease" then I know what you're going through. Dis-ease is

literally just that—when our body or mind is no longer in a state of ease.

My name is Jennifer Bitner, and I've had an extensive journey in the last 13 years with chronic anxiety and panic attacks, so I know what it feels like to lose all hope for a quality life. I also overcame this adversity, so I know what it's like to recover and rediscover life through a whole new lens.

Flashback to 2006: after three years of struggling with what I thought was severe food intolerances (due to my stomach always being in knots and feeling like I always had to run to a bathroom), I was actually diagnosed with an anxiety disorder. *A what? But I'm a pageant girl with amazing friends, an awesome boyfriend and a great family. Why is something wrong with me?* At the age of 22 I'd never heard of anxiety disorders before, and to be honest, there were not a lot of places to turn to for help. Unlike the availability that saturated the physical health industry, resources for mental health conditions were scarce.

My friends had never spoken about this "anxiety" thing and my parents didn't know how to deal with me. I didn't really know where to turn.

Well, if you are one of those people suffering, I want to let you know there's nothing to be ashamed of! It's totally normal and okay! There are ways to take corrective action to lead you to a balanced life again.

My mission is to remove the stigma surrounding mental health disorders and to highlight the importance of creating a healthy mind. There should be as much social acceptance around gaining a fit and healthy mind as there is around physical fitness (gaining a healthier body).

I challenge you to ask someone what comes to mind when they hear the words "physical health." I bet they would rattle off things like, "strength," "fit," "healthy," "in shape," etc. Now if you ask them what comes to mind when they hear the words "mental health," they might be more inclined to respond with words like, "disease," "illness," "crazy," "depressed," etc.

Isn't it interesting how we associate mental health as a state of illness, instead of as a state of optimal wellness, which it truly is?

I am here to advocate for equality between physical and mental health, so everyone can live with a sense of hope for recovery. Having worked in the physical fitness industry for over a decade, I experienced firsthand the positive associations physical health has in our society. I saw how there were amazing programs offered to help people live a fit and healthy life through movement. On the other hand, mental health was a whole other ball game, and in 2006 I became the new captain for that team.

This is why I started my company, My Mind Fitness, back in 2012. I knew one day I would be one of the greatest advocates for mental wellbeing. I knew that one day I would be recovered from this debilitating disorder and live free. I knew I was going to do BIG things in the mental health space. I just knew that being a catalyst to change the perception of mental wellness would be my purpose. I just had to free myself first.

At the time, the best thing I could offer during my recovery stage was to publish a blog with all the ah-ha moments I had, the words of wisdom I could share, lessons I had learned along my journey, and the perils I had endured. I took those blog posts down a few years ago when I launched my website into a coaching practice, but I kept them for something special.

That something special is this book.

Each chapter in this book will take you through a season of my mental health journey, followed by a few of the sacred blog posts that I wrote during that specific time along my path. Each chapter ends with a Mind Fitness Challenge that I invite you to participate in so you can start your own mind fitness journey. You'll also find a journaling section at the back of the book to take notes on some the actions steps you'll want to take.

I believe too many people suffer in silence with mental health disorders. Why? Two reasons: one, you can hide it; and two, there is such a strong stigma associated with not being in a state of optimal mental health. You may not be able to hide physical health conditions, but you can put a smile on your face even when you're breaking down inside. That's the difference between physical and mental fitness: one is quite noticeable while the other is often hidden—yet both are equally important to living a healthy life.

I came to find that there are very simple, basic solutions to living an overall healthier, peaceful life. The mind is an incredibly powerful tool that needs to be fit and healthy to make changes possible in any other aspect of your life.

I now refer to myself as a Mind Fitness Warrior after battling some of the deepest valleys in my life with mental health, and rising up on the other side as a stronger, more powerful person for it.

During my journey, I became a Certified Professional Coach, a Reiki Practitioner (energy healing), Neuro-Linguistic Programming Practitioner (language of the mind) and a self-proclaimed mind-enthusiast. I co-hosted my own iTV show, *Mind Fitness*, and launched an online interview series on YouTube called *Mind Fitness Warriors*. I am also one of the top-ranked educators globally on aromatherapy, using plant-based medicine for emotional wellness.

I have researched abundantly on the mind and brain, as well as the connection our different body systems have to our overall wellbeing.

Let's just say, I'm really happy you opened this book and will be starting your own journey towards a fit & healthy mind!

Not only do I want to take you through my personal story, but I also want to share with you my recovery and what worked for me. It may not be the answer for everyone, but if you can feel a sense of belonging and ease just from knowing how you and your journey are gifts, then the purpose for me writing this book has been fulfilled.

I will tell you, I write with passion and humour and what you're reading is my own personal thoughts, journaling, and opinions. I'm no doctor and I'm not here to replace medical advice or tell you what's right for you. These are my experiences and they are what led me to a life of pure freedom—no PhD required. That being said, I like to think I'm pretty well-versed in the mental health department.

I have learned to be comical about my experience, as I believe life should be lived with lightness and playfulness wherever it can be.

So sit back, grab a tea, and feel free to make light of it along with me.

Chapter 1

Where It All Began

Potty Talk

Well, no more wasting time with the warm up, let me dive right in. The beginning of my story is in 2002 during my first year of university. I struggled with social anxiety around … get this … the dreaded dun dun dun … BATHROOM (or the loo for any Brits reading, washroom/restroom for my Americans). In any sense of the word, it scared the crap out of me (for real!) to not have access to one.

That's right. A topic most people never talk about because it's not ladylike or coffee-convo worthy, I feared to the depths of my being. Try being a pageant girl modelling an "all together" kind of life while being brutally fearful of not having access to a bathroom.

Weird, isn't it?

Well there's a reason for this phobia, but you'll have to keep reading the book to find out (cue suspense music).

So yes, I hid this bathroom phobia from everyone.
I had to structure my days around where bathrooms were and eat only at certain times so I wouldn't have to worry about needing one. Throughout my three years at university it only got worse (and I only got better at hiding it). I wound up needing special permission to write my exams in a private room so I didn't have the social embarrassment

of getting up in front of hundreds of people *if* I had to go to the bathroom.

I even dropped out of my 10:00AM Criminology class because the exit was right beside the lecturing professor and *everyone* would see me leaving at 10:20 every morning when I needed to get up to go to the bathroom. I actually subconsciously trained my body to believe it had to go at exactly 10:20AM *only* during that specific class. It really shows the power of our mind-body connection and how it can deceive us.

I also skillfully mastered how to ensure no one could hear me when I went into the bathroom. I found them in the most inconspicuous places where most people didn't go just so I could hide.

I remember going to the university medical centre about why my stomach was always in knots and why I kept feeling this urgency for a bathroom. This is when they diagnosed me with IBS, Irritable Bowel Syndrome. Looking back now, it was actually my binge eating and severe nervousness that were the culprits. I wouldn't eat all day to avoid needing a bathroom, then stuff my face when I got home, and this vicious cycle wreaked havoc on my poor body. I preferred to just try to cope or manage the moments on my own, but when you stay silent about your struggles, no one can really help you get better, hence my misdiagnosis.

Am I alone in this phobia? Any other bathroom-a-holics out there with this obsession?

I even remember the bathroom at my then boyfriend's house being right beside the kitchen and living room. Because my belief was that there *had* to be microphones concealed in the floors and ceilings of everyone's powder rooms, I just couldn't bring myself to enter that room of pending social judgment. Unless, of course, I brought a blender in with me to mask the sound of me tinkling (because everyone whips up a smoothie while taking a pee). Totally kidding, I didn't go to that length, but I can't tell you how many times I perfectly staged needing to run a shower or blow dry my hair at other people's houses. Let's not even talk about the facade I had of an addiction to Starbucks coffee, and *only* Starbucks coffee, just so I could leave the house for java and a quiet, individual person, sound proof potty room.

Until this point, my bathroom phobia was more of a severe social embarrassment issue.

As I sit here writing this, my little inner voice is saying, *Jen, do you really want to publish this? Talking about your bathroom phobia? What will people think about you? Everyone will laugh!*

Which is why you're reading this right now. No more questioning whether your journey is crazy, shameful or embarrassing. Let's just be real folks—life ain't always sunshine and rainbows!

What Someone Else Thinks of You Is None of Your Business

In life you have to remember that you can't control what other people think or say about you. No matter how hard you try to be what the world wants you to be, there will be someone out there who doesn't appreciate your efforts to conform. After years of trying to be the best "this and that," I realized that I could only be happy if I was the best version of myself. The only person you can compare yourself to is who you were yesterday.

If you're being bullied or mistreated, taken advantage of, or unappreciated, you have to ask yourself, *what am I living for—their approval or my own happiness?*

Bullies are bullies because they have their own demons they are living with, and knowing *you* are going to feel pain too makes them feel pleasure.

Remember this prayer written by the American theologian Reinhold Niebuhr:

> "God grant me the Serenity to accept the things I cannot change, the Courage to change the things I can, and the Wisdom to know the difference"

(I live by this prayer, which is why I had *Serenity* tattooed on my left wrist!)

Always know it takes peace within you to accept the things and people you can't change. Worry about you and what makes you happy. Be mindful to appreciate those who treat you right and accept you for who you are. Those people are easy to overlook while trying to prove your true beauty to someone who doesn't care to see it.

The Right "What Ifs"

Those who struggle living in a world of "what ifs" know how hard it is to kick the habit of worrying about hypothetical scenarios that all point in the direction of *I'm doomed.*

I discovered an amazing way to flip this question, which almost always creates the unnecessary anxiety of future negative or catastrophic possibilities, we always ask ourselves.

Anxious worriers are always thinking about future events that may cause a panic attack or anxiety if they came true: *What if it's crowded and I panic then we have to leave and everyone will stare at me? What if there's no exit? What if I start getting anxious and have to leave in the middle of dinner ... what will everyone think? What if I feel stuck and have a panic attack?* What if, what if, what if. Worriers always put their "what ifs" into a negative thought. This pattern of thought becomes a habit in your brain wiring. You start to filter events into a series of, *how can this go wrong*, and then you notice all the ways it won't work out well for you. Then, without fail, once the event is present, you bring to life all those thoughts. What you think, you become; your thoughts become your actions and your reality.

Have you ever heard of your RAS? It's the Reticular Activating System. This is like a filter that works in your brain. It weeds out information you don't need, and it processes and recognizes bits of information that match with what your conscious mind is looking for. Ever notice how after you just finished telling your best friend about your dream car, you see that exact car passing you by every time you go for a drive? All of a sudden everyone has that car! You never saw it before, but now you see it all the time.

This is because your RAS is taking that sensory information and sending it to your conscious awareness because it knows you are keen on that specific vehicle. When it came to my anxiety, my brain was communicating with my conscious mind around bathrooms, letting it know whenever I was in a situation where there was potential social embarrassment (which, for me, was any situation where I didn't have immediate access to one and might need it).

We fear that if we don't prepare ourselves in advance for the possibility of feeling anxious, then we are unprotected if we are faced with an unexpected situation.

We protect ourselves with these plans of what we'll do if something happens—our exit strategies. What I've learned is that it's certainly okay to have a plan in place, but once you have that plan, only focus on the positive "what if" scenarios from there.

What if you tried this technique and it worked? What if it changed the way you think and now you go into situations feeling calm and relaxed? What if it helped you create a healthier mind? Hmmm … What if …

Mind Fitness Challenge:

I challenge you to a twist in your pattern. What if every time you thought "what if," it's a positive thought? *What if when we get there I feel calm and relaxed? What if I feel totally comfortable in the crowd of people and I realize how safe and at ease I am? What if during dinner I am having such a great time that I just enjoy myself, and I stay throughout the entire evening with no issues? What if I just feel powerfully perfect? What if this business deal ends up going through and I land the job!?*

When that future event arises, the thought pattern you'll recall is the one you trained yourself to feel calm and relaxed about. When you bring forward these consistent thoughts, your actions become calm and relaxed. If you spend ample time foreseeing calmness and relaxation, then there is no other thought impulse for your mind and body. Once you've formed this habit, negative thoughts of the future will decrease. You'll recognize that you don't have to plan for unforeseen events because you understand how to be calm and relaxed in your mind and body.

You'll also notice that as you anticipate positivity in the future, your whole energy shifts. You start to smile more often, look forward to upcoming events, and even feel the change in your body as you repeatedly focus on the enjoyment of the future.

Chapter 2

The Diagnosis

The Stop Light Trauma

It was spring 2006, six months after starting my big-girl career with the largest fitness chain in Canada, when my first actual panic attack happened.

My then boyfriend and I had just eaten fast food at the mall. I remember thinking to myself as we left for the parking lot, *Oh boy, my stomach doesn't feel right.* Almost immediately after pulling out of the mall, my stomach became upset and I seriously needed a bathroom.

I told my boyfriend he needed to pull over and get me to a bathroom STAT!

Unfortunately, we were in bumper-to-bumper traffic with no option of pulling over or getting anywhere fast.

All I could see were the red brake lights in front of me and red stoplights that had a lineup of at least 25 cars before we could get through.

Thoughts began running through my head faster than I could make sense of, *Uh oh, where are you going to go? You need a bathroom fast, hurry, find one! What will happen if you don't? What are you going to do? Why is this stoplight red for so long? When is the light going to go green?! Another red light? Are we ever going to get through this damn stoplight?!?!*

I started to feel my hands get sweaty.

My heart started racing a mile a minute.

My eyes were scanning the scene at the speed of light, looking for any opportunities for me to jump out the car and race to safety.

I started rambling and grabbing on to the handle on the ceiling of my car. I was flailing my hands, like an irate Italian *nonna*, begging my boyfriend to get me somewhere FAST!

There was nothing he could do—we were stuck. He started getting frustrated, telling me to calm down and stop freaking out. Side note: never tell someone who is panicking to calm down. Just don't.

Tears started rolling down my face. I could see it—my greatest social fear was about to take place in this car. Right here, right now. *Well, good luck ever living this one down, Jen.*

My panic continued to rise, my stomach clenched like I had the worst flu bug imaginable. My heart at this point felt like was was going to jump right out of my chest. My breath was quick and rapid.
The last lane of cars made it through the advanced green light and it was finally our turn to GO! Burning rubber, we pulled into the first plaza. Finally reaching a bathroom at a pizza joint, I locked myself inside and had no idea what I had just experienced. Well, it turns out that I just had my first panic attack. It took hours for my adrenaline to level out, at which point I crashed.
I hoped it was over, but unfortunately, that was just the beginning for me.

I remember heading home later that evening, and as I approached the very first stoplight, my stomach sank, my hands got sweaty again and those same thoughts started running through my head. *Uh oh, you're stuck at a red light again. What are you going to do? What if you have to go again? How are you going to get out of this car?*

It was like a horrible nightmare replaying itself over and over.

The stoplight trauma proceeded to cause me panic attacks every time I stepped into a car and saw brake lights or stopped at a red light. The distance that used to take me five minutes to drive to work was now taking 20 minutes because I would pull over at a coffee shop and again at a gas station because I thought I had to go to the bathroom.

The memory was so heavily engrained in my psyche, that subconsciously I was avoiding any instance in which I would be at risk of being in traffic, in an effort to dodge a panic attack. This is what is commonly referred to as Post Traumatic Stress Disorder (PTSD).

You're probably thinking PTSD is only for the strongest of soldiers or those who have been through something serious like abuse or tragedy, but, my friends, don't downplay what you've been through. Chronic stress caused by a traumatic event in your past is a real thing. It's also something we can work to reverse the response to, so once it is acknowledged we can begin to heal.

At the time my panic attacks began, I was about six months into my new job and was not about to ruin my new success because of this inconvenient traumatic experience.
I was top in the country for sales and on a mission to climb the corporate ladder fast. I didn't have time or energy for this stupid phobia.

On top of it all, I worked for the largest chain of fitness clubs in Canada, so I felt as though I needed to be a confident portrayal of health and wellness. That's another reason why I hid it for so long. I feared that if I was pegged with a health problem I would lose credibility in selling health memberships.

The episodes kept happening and were getting worse. A couple months following the stop light trauma, I finally opened up to my mom about what I was experiencing. She convinced me to see my family doctor, leading me straight into the world of mental health.

The Stigma Is Real, Yo!

My doctor made an educated guess that what I was experiencing was anxiety and gave me a referral to the Adult Mental Health Clinic to see a specialist.

What?! Mental Health Clinic?? But I'm not crazy. I'm not depressed. I'm not a nut-bar. Why do I need to go to a mental health anything?!

At the time, this was my own personal perception of mental health.

But I went.

On my first visit I walked in and noticed how the room was cold and grey. The posters on the walls were all of people who looked sad and lonely. The lady behind the glass counter was very monotone and clinical. I sat down beside another girl around my age who looked incredibly unhappy. I immediately realized I didn't belong here. *This isn't me. I'm fine! I'm ok!* I didn't want to associate myself with this place. I was scared and fearful of the judgment and labelling, so I tried to pretend I was an intern waiting for an interview, hoping no one thought I was there actually seeking "help." It was hard for me to think that my career was dedicated to supporting those who wanted to start a physical health journey in a place that was upbeat, fun, social, and high energy, but there I was, cursing that my condition was mental. If this is the only kind of support available for mental health, then I figured I wouldn't last too long.

During my first visit I was diagnosed with a severe anxiety and panic disorder, received the recommendation that I should be on anti-anxiety medication, I was set up with a weekly appointment with a counsellor to work on coping mechanisms.

The next week I ended up meeting this new counsellor. I called her Dr. Jane (even though she wasn't a doctor). She became my everything for that next year. My confidante, my hope, my person to dump all my feelings on. Every Tuesday at 2:30PM for a whole year I sat in her little office with a big window, overlooking a sea of other corporate buildings, thinking to myself, *today will be the day she fixes me.* I wish I could say my anxiety vanished one day when she finally gave me the magic technique I had been hoping for, but then this would make for a really short book, wouldn't it? So I kept going faithfully, week after week. Often, I would show up simply because it felt good to have someone to pour everything out to.

In order to stay in this program with Dr. Jane, once a month I had to see a psychiatrist. Every visit, this older gentlemen, who seemed like he was a few years overdue for retirement, tried to push a new prescription on me. I remember one visit he highly recommended something for Adult ADHD after I mentioned how I couldn't focus during the team meetings at work. There may have been more to that assessment, but I just knew I didn't want to alter my personality with meds any more than I already was. I also wasn't keen on the idea of being jacked up on pills for every aspect of my life that wasn't functioning "perfectly."

I did agree to start a new medication for the panic attacks and anxiety, because this was affecting my quality of life. I have to say, those little white pills helped take the edge off a bit, but they were very addictive and still not addressing the root cause.

After requesting to see a new therapist (who would ideally put more effort into finding a solution other than medication) I found myself in a session with this woman who kept asking me over and over again, "Do you have *any* reason to believe you will not make it to a bathroom in time? Has it ever happened that you *did not* make it in time, and that embarrassed you, and that's what has caused this fear of bathrooms?"

Each time she asked I said no.

She asked again. I looked down at my folded hands, and firmly said, "NO!"

She then told me if I wasn't being honest with her, she couldn't help me.

What did this lady want from me? I told her no. That's all I had for her. A big NO.

I remember this moment with my therapist because of how it made me feel. I sensed my resistance every time I said no to her, but I wasn't quite sure why. I would have this flash back moment to when I was a little girl, but I had so much shame attached to it that I couldn't bring myself to talk about it (you'll learn more about this later).

Over the course of the year at the Adult Mental Health Clinic, seeing multiple therapists, Dr. Jane, and being on the meds, I didn't seem to be getting anywhere near recovery.

After a couple of years of pulling the car over at almost every gas station or coffee shop to run to a bathroom, my anxiety got worse and started happening anywhere I felt I couldn't easily access a bathroom if I needed one (not just in cars anymore).

I made fewer plans to go out with friends, I avoided road trips and going to someone's house where there was only one bathroom (in case someone went in it because, of course, I would "need" it desperately all of a sudden).

I had to make up so many excuses whenever I would wind up in a situation that would trigger my anxiety. I can't tell you how many family functions I faked food poisoning or the flu, just so I could leave. Or how many holiday dinners I refused to eat because I didn't want to trigger my anxiety.

I had a fear of needing to go to the bathroom which caused anxiety, and one of the side effects of anxiety is the need to go to the bathroom. So it was a vicious cycle that never ended.

The only thing I looked forward to during the week was bedtime, when I could finally lie down for eight hours without a panic attack.

My Friday and Saturday nights were spent completely obliterated drunk, and Sundays were spent recovering from a massive hangover. Drinking excessively was the only thing that could numb the pain of a week's worth of high flight-or-fight responses and chronic anxiety attacks.

When Can I Expect to Be Free from Anxiety?

I get this question a lot. Here's the thing … anxiety is a basic human emotion. It's your body's response mechanism to a perceived threat or danger that automatically kicks in when your brain signals to your adrenals, "Let's go, she's afraid! We need to release the soldiers and prep her for attack!" You can't possibly get *rid* of this natural human instinct, it's there to serve and protect you.

What we can do is train our mind to properly perceive life situations so it doesn't send the signal unnecessarily. That's where having a fit and healthy mind comes into play. Once we learn how to properly categorize our thoughts, learn how to do positive self-talk, re-direct negative thought patterns, and unwire connections that have been made to past fearful situations, then we can control when we really need to "release the soldiers."

Remember, anxiety is a defence mechanism. Its sole purpose is to protect you, so it's your responsibility to know when you are truly in danger. Those of us who send false alarms to our poor little soldiers all the time suffer the most. We live in what I call "crisis mode" all day. Our bodies never have a chance to rest because we are always worried about what the next threatening situation is going to be and if we are going to be able to get through it.

So to answer the question, "When will I get over my anxiety?" The answer is never. You can't eliminate the emotion from your DNA. We can, however, exercise our minds to learn how to use this mechanism for its true intended purpose. This training will take time. For me, it took a lot of time. But I appreciate every little thing it has taught me along the way.

I believe a mental health journey is more than just about achieving a strong and healthy mind; it's about who you become in the process. Something that's really cool about going through this process—and I do promise you there are positive sides to this—is that you'll develop an inner strength that others will never have the chance to understand or experience. Someone who suffers from generalized anxiety has such a heightened awareness of their mind and body that accomplishing things they fear can be a massive achievement.

Mind Fitness Challenge:

Journal about all the ways you've noticed strength appear from your journey. Really think about it. How have you become a stronger version of yourself? What have you had to endure that has now given you extra armour? What have you learned about your mind-body connection? It's important to take a step aside to look at the positive lessons and growth opportunities within the journey that seemingly breaks us down. I promise if you really try to see it, the achievements are there and you should be proud!

Chapter 3

The Turning Point

Surfers Paradise or Hell?

In January 2009, three years after my first panic attack, I took a leave of absence from my job as a general manager of a fitness club and travelled to Australia. Obviously, if you're nervous about being without access to a bathroom, you hop on a 26-hour plane ride across the world with hundreds of people sharing a few tiny bathroom stalls. Perfect idea.

But I didn't want to stop my life. I wanted to go soul searching as most 24 year olds yearn to do!

On this trip I experienced the turning point of my severe anxiety disorder.

I remember one specific day that shifted everything.

I was attempting to take public transit to one of the local beaches in Surfers Paradise. I got to the bus stop outside my residence, but my anxiety was so bad that I kept running back to the house to go to the bathroom (well not actually go but just to calm my nerves and prove to myself I didn't have to go).
I arrived at the beach a few hours later. I didn't eat or drink a thing the whole time I was there so I could make it home without feeling the need for a rest stop.

Once I decided to leave the beach, the anxiety kicked in again.

I got on the bus and the panic got worse and worse with every passing minute. I finally jumped out of my seat, ran to the front of the bus and yelled at the driver, "PULL OVER!" He was taken off guard by my demand and pulled the bus over in the middle of a residential area, which was a two hour walk from where I was staying.

I got off even though he warned me I would be lost. I walked back with the sun burning my skin, in tears at the thought of why my life turned out this way. *I'm so young, I can't live the rest of my life dreading every single day and every event outside the safety of my home.* That two-hour walk gave me a lot to think about.

Enough was enough.

As soon as I got back (after getting some cool cloths for my blistering, sunburned shoulders and feet) I googled "anxiety disorder." In 2009, Google wasn't as common as it is now for diagnosing your feelings.

But lo and behold, I found a program that would be the catalyst for shifting my recovery from a medical approach (talk therapy and medication) to a holistic lifestyle approach. The program was eight weeks of self-directed meditation, relaxation techniques (which I had never attempted before), nutrition guidance, and other simple but powerfully effective lifestyle changes that brought my body and mind back into harmony.

I immediately purchased it, downloaded it, and got it printed and bound the next day.

This became the first, and most amazing, program I ever took. It is called Panic Away by Barry McDonagh, if you ever want to look it up. Here is an excerpt I summarized from the manual, which does a great job of explaining anxiety:

—

Anxiety is one of the most basic of all emotions and although it's unpleasant, it's in no means harmful. It's defined as a state of apprehension or fear resulting from the anticipation of a real or imagined threat, event or situation. General Anxiety Disorder (GAD) is essentially the feeling of lingering anxiety accompanied by anxious thoughts and this can last throughout the day. It often means excessive worry or tension about health, money, family or work. Panic attacks will typically initiate a period of general anxiety up to days after the attack because it causes such confusion and fear in the body, which is a breeding ground for anxiety.

Some people may only experience panic attacks, whereas others may have general anxiety and never an attack. One may experience these as situational or spontaneous. Situational meaning you've had one out of the blue and now you fear places or situations that you associate with that original panic attack.

—

I was ready. I was excited. I was hopeful.

I started to experience some really great changes while I was away. I started to feel my body restore a bit of calm. I started to feel more in control. I started to understand *why* my mind was going through this vicious, fearful cycle. I gained more compassion for my body.
For the first time, I felt that there was light at the end of the tunnel.

My First Relapse

When I returned home from Australia, I went back to my role as a manager working long hours in a very stimulating environment. I also went back to drinking loads on the weekends and running on coffee. With no surprise to me now, my panic attacks and chronic anxiety came back–and they came back with a vengeance. Almost like my body was saying, "We were doing so well, why'd you go and throw it all away!"

After a few months back home, my boyfriend, Dave (who is now my husband), said, "Jen, when you were in Australia, you were doing so well. What were you doing?"

It clicked.

I remembered how good I felt.

I decided to give myself eight weeks again and go back through the Panic Away program. Instead of giving up, thinking I would never get better, I decided to get back on the horse (that's a saying, right?). I even took a few vacation days to stay home to reread and redo the program.

I started to slowly regain some of my emotional balance. But it was nowhere near the healing I had hoped for to live a *normal* healthy life.

At the time, I didn't connect the work stress I was under at home to my anxiety, versus the more relaxed environment when I was abroad.

For the next couple years, I tried numerous programs and went to around 40 different practitioners to try to rid myself of this frustrating condition. I tried everything from medication, hypnosis, therapy,

Cognitive Behavioural Therapy (CBT), and Neuro-Linguistic Programming (NLP) to Reiki, mediums, meditation, diets, etc. I wanted to experience all the different options out there that are geared towards mental wellness. I was powering through different healers, different theories, and different approaches like it was my job!

No seriously, the amount of time I spent seeking answers was probably comparable to a part-time gig—except I was investing money instead of making it!

At this point, I realized that I was making steps in the right direction and I had to be okay with all the pieces not being perfectly lined up just yet.

I had to remind myself quite often, *It's coming. Hang tight.*

It's Not a Setback; It's a Time Out

Often we get very frustrated on our journey because out of nowhere, BAM!

Our progress goes from one step forward to two steps back. Just because we have a setback along our journey, like an episode or panic attack, after such great progression, doesn't mean we are all of a sudden pulling a U-turn. To be honest, I don't even like the word setback—it implies going in the wrong direction.

We are human; there are times our bodies will revert to old behaviours or do what comes easiest and natural. That's okay. That's normal. Sometimes it's actually worth something.

Most often I find when the body throws itself into a panic attack or you get anxiety, it's the body's way of telling you to slow down and pay attention. If you stop and take a moment to reflect on what's happening in the present, you'll most likely find there's some sort of answer to why you're sending your nerves on a marathon. For me, it use to be that I would forget to eat properly, hadn't meditated in a while, or hadn't exercised my mind or body ... regardless, there is always some lesson or reason as to why I'd have to take a time out.

In any event, it's *not* taking any steps back in progression towards a healthier mind; you just may not be doing the right things to move it forward in that moment.

Think of it like you lost a bunch of weight and then some old habits creep their way back into the present. Chances are you would put back on a couple pounds. In that case—RED FLAG—your body is reacting to the unhealthy eating and reminding you it can't use certain foods for fuel. It doesn't mean you're destined to gain all the weight back. It's just giving you a reminder that you have the skills necessary to kick those bad habits and continue on your healthy journey.

Episodes are just reminders to take a breather, check in with what your body needs, and move forward with the right plan.

Grab Your Water Wings!

Contrary to the advice of most of the medical practitioners or therapists I went to, I personally am a huge advocate for having a crutch to get you through the toughest part of your journey—challenging your biggest fear or obstacle.

Some may say a crutch makes you dependent, but I say if it helps you still live your life then go for it!

I was often told by those who cared about me most, "Don't take pills with you, that's only furthering your need for dependency. You shouldn't be relying on something, this is in your head and you need to just change your thoughts." Well, every time I tried to just jump into a fearful situation with no water wings, I sank. I think it's okay to start off with baby steps and work your way from the flotation device, to a doggie paddle, to swimming laps on your own.

Let me use the example of a crutch that helped me at the beginning of my recovery.

My brother-in-law came up with the idea of a pop n' squat! So whenever I went in the car I brought a box or mini potty in case we got stuck somewhere with no bathrooms. Did I ever need to use it? No. That's not the point—I felt safe knowing it was there. For the better part of my journey this helped me move through the fear. It was my little peace of mind. It allowed me to still do the things that would normally freak me right out and throw me into a panic attack (long drives, road trips, plane rides), and got me beyond the comfort zone of my house. I could go out and do all the things I wanted to do, just in a way that made me still mildly comfortable.

I remember there being times where I had really heightened anxiety and an event outside of my comfort zone that I wanted to attend would be happening, for example a night out on the town with the girls in limos. Did I say, "No, sorry, I'm afraid I'll have a panic attack?" Nope—I got myself in my own car and went! I may not have driven with everyone else, but I still went! Or if the girls were getting hotel rooms, did I not stay over because there's only one bathroom?

No. I would just get a room with only one other person instead of five!

So don't feel as though you're expected to get from A-Z overnight. If there's something that makes you comfortable that will allow you to push the limits and get out of your safe zone to live your life, then do it!

Grab your water wings and jump on into the water!

Once you gain the confidence from repetition of a formerly feared or anxiety-inducing situation, which now no longer causes you anxiety, you will see that you may not even need to bring/use your water wings anymore. It's like a child and their soother—you WILL grow out of it. I promise.

I Want It ALL

It's important to have goals, dreams, and desires for the way we want our lives to be. Our passions are what keep us motivated and driven for the amazing things that are destined in our lives. There's only one catch—you may not have it all at once. So, don't beat yourself up with the, "Woe is me, nothing can ever be perfect in my life!" because it likely won't be the way you want it all at the same time.

Ever notice that if work is going amazing, another area in your life starts to needs some TLC? Or you find that amazing partner and then your career path is not what you wanted it to be? To "have it all" is something reality TV has exposed as a fantasy. Even celebrities don't have it all! There will always be something that needs work or change. The only constant thing in life is change. There will always be something in your life that you need to dedicate effort and energy to make better. Be okay with working on you and your journey for the rest of your life … and make it fun! Be completely and utterly grateful for the way things are today—perfectly imperfect as they may be!

I call this the 80/20 rule. There's often 20% of your life, partner, or job that you may not find perfect or the way you wish it to be. You have to be able to look beyond the small imperfections and see the greater picture. Allow the 80% to be enough for you to be at peace and grateful. Accept life for what it is and love and embrace all the amazing aspects of it. Soon enough you'll notice that 20% start to get smaller as you're no longer focusing on what's not right. It's about accepting the imperfections as part of the whole. I always used to say my greatest strength is that I have the ability to do anything I want; my greatest weakness is that I want to do it all at right now.

Sometimes we need to recognize that although our minds have this incredible power to dream big, push through adversity, and overcome struggles and obstacles, there are effects on our emotional and physical self when we over-do it. Sure we'd all love to have that major promotion and climb the corporate ladder for the title; the brand new fully furnished home with white picket fence; that dreamy amazing soul mate who'll give us everything we need; and a brand new dream car *right now* because, let's face it, we work hard so we deserve it, right?

The truth of the matter is that it's amazing to desire these new aspects to our lifestyle, but to have it all right now is simply unrealistic and takes a major toll on us emotionally and physically when we try to accomplish it all today. And to be honest, it probably wouldn't be fun. If you did get everything you dreamed of right now, you would have nothing to work for and that would become boring.

Here's my advice. Just like juggling five balls in the air for the first time, one of them is bound to drop at some point, and it's exhausting trying to keep them all up together. So instead, pick one ball up at a time and learn to toss it back and forth. Work on it, work towards mastering it, put your energy into it. Once you have effortlessly mastered the one-ball toss, pick up the next one and begin to juggle two. Eventually you will master two, and then three, and so on. You work towards the skills of becoming a master by practicing diligently.

So pick the most important life change or goal you have and focus on it. It's more effective to keep most things in your life stable while you make a major change. This will help keep your anxiety levels down, and rest your body and emotional energy so you're ready to give your new journey your all.

A business coach once taught me this and it always stuck, just FOCUS: Focus One Course Until Success.

Granted, when working on a certain goal there are going to be other positive changes that you'll naturally want to focus on along the way. Take starting a physical fitness journey for example. When you embark on this journey you will also be more open to making positive changes to your nutrition, stress management, sleep, and mental health, just to name a few.

So, YES you can certainly have it all … at different points in life. Just be patient. Life isn't a birthday party with all your gifts on one day; it's a series of special occasions where you can celebrate and appreciate your next big thing. Keep that party hat close—you'll be bringing it out for the rest of your life!

Bonus Travelling Tips

Here's some advice for those of you who suffer from major anxiety when travelling. Having travelled to Australia and gone on countless other trips during the most heightened times of my anxiety, I discovered quite a few things about what to do and what not to do. First off, if you're recovering and trying to restore balance in your life right now, perhaps space out your getaways so you're not overloaded with stimuli all at once.

I remember booking a huge three-day party weekend getaway, followed by a weekend for my 30th birthday in Vegas. Back to Back. Yikes.

Having two weekends in hotels, eating out, and doing activities beyond my normal level of action was very exhausting.

What happens when our bodies are exhausted? We become vulnerable. What happens when we become vulnerable? We are more prone to anxiety or panic attacks. Luckily for me, I was seasoned in my practice by this point and had huge awareness of my body, so I took some outs that made me more comfortable (I walked a lot of places instead of cabbing and limited the number of nights where partying would get out of control). But if you're just beginning your journey I recommend taking it slower.

When you really think about it, if we're moving towards restoring our balance, then partying a lot, drinking alcohol, and eating processed foods are not helping us whether we suffer from an unhealthy mental state or not. Anyone who is on a journey (physical included) will benefit from a more peaceful flow.

So what can we do when travelling so we can still have fun?

Stay Hydrated and Get Rest

When we are dehydrated or exhausted our bodies can become shaky and sensitive (even at a mild dehydration of 1%). These sensations can mimic those of anxiety and send us for a false ride down fear lane. Even though we're not fearful of anything in particular in that moment, our bodies are giving us those anxious feelings and we'll react accordingly.

Same goes for being hung-over. As our bodies are recovering from a wild night, they are sending off sensations and signals that make it hard for us to recognize whether it's anxiety or just a hang-over, so of course, our natural reaction is to answer anxiety's call. This can potentially throw us into "panic mode."

Make a Plan and Stick to It—Don't Over Analyze

If it makes you comfortable to think about the routes you're going to take, or what you are going to wear so you feel more comfortable, or how you want to get to and from places, then think of it once, set it as your plan, and let it be. The more you obsess about the process of travelling and thinking about all the "what ifs," the more you are putting those fearful thoughts into action. Plan out how you ideally would want it to work out and leave it. The energy you put out into the universe will become your reality. If you think about it not working out, it won't. If you think about it being a safe and comfortable ride, it will be. Your wish is the Universe's command.

Eat Well

You are what you eat. Really. When I'm away I love to let loose and indulge in all the yummy food. Let me remind you that so many foods are intolerable to our bodies and over doing it on the dairy and gluten, for example, can cause us to feel inflamed and off. I know when I eat out often I end up having an upset stomach, which triggers those anxious sensations in my body.

So when I'm away, I have to be conscious of what I'm fuelling my body with. Sticking to as much water, protein, veggies, and whole foods (unprocessed) as possible, allows my body to stay balanced with no food reactions. The more balanced I am while away, the more positive energy I have to put towards the other areas that might slip while having a good time!

Don't get me wrong—I still indulge here and there, we're just talking about being more aware of how often we indulge, and if our bodies are asking for a rest.

In the end, the goal is to never let thoughts or past fears prevent us from doing anything we want to do.

On this journey, I've learned that every time you step outside your comfort zone you add another notch of success to your belt. Even if you hit a few bumps along the road or slip up with your balance, you still should make amazing memories. And guess what … I'm here to write about it, which means there was really nothing to fear. Go figure.

Mind Fitness Challenge:

Write down what your ideal day looks like when it comes to being balanced. What do you eat? How many hours do you sleep? What are the events of the day? How does this make you feel? You may want to create an "avoid list" of things you note that cause you discomfort—like alcoholic drinks, coffee, inadequate sleep, etc. Start to recognize what feeling good looks like and what imbalance looks like so you can become the boss of your emotional wellness.

Chapter 4

If It's Meant to Be, It's Up to Me

Who Finally Saved Me

Through my persistence in finding a "cure" I dabbled in so many different modalities and alternatives that I started to realize they were all pointing in one direction: There is no *external* cure.

No magic pill, doctor, practitioner, or course.

Through all the work, the healing, the road to recovery, the real answer was clear. The change needed to happen within *myself*.

I had to choose to do the work every damn day. I had to purposefully make changes, not just show up to an appointment with a specialist and expect to walk out a new person.

I had to do a lot of work to undo a lot of unhealthy habits and brain wiring.

In 2011, a year before my wedding date, I committed to radical change. I decided to take a holistic and natural approach to completely overhaul my lifestyle to become a stronger, healthier version of myself. I was determined to take my health into my own hands and get well.

I started with a naturopathic doctor and a holistic nutritionist. I took my personal training workouts more seriously and started a course in mediation, got certified in energy healing, and a lot of the modalities that helped me, so I could use them more consistently, then help others.

The change started happening. I was feeling brighter, more fulfilled, and less anxious with fewer panic attacks.

Don't get me wrong—I still had my moments. I still had to accommodate myself with bathrooms in some scenarios and still had bad days, but they were less frequent. I was also still in a career that had me working extreme hours and I still enjoyed my drinking on the weekends. So parts of my lifestyle were still not conducive to full recovery, but at this point, I knew I was going in the right direction. I was happy to see and feel the change, even if it was slower than it could have been.

I had to accept that even though I felt like I had been going through the same lessons repeatedly, it was for a reason.

That being said, I felt I was taking the steps as I was meant to take them.

One at a time.

Enrolled in the School of Life

Do you ever feel as though you're faced with the same situation over and over again and you don't know why? Why does this keep happening to you? Why do you keep going through the same thing time and time again?

Here's the deal—life will keep bringing you the same test over and over again until you pass it. It's part of being enrolled in the school of life. Next time you find you're facing a scenario similar to one you've faced in the past, don't run. Just stay put and deal. The hard fact is that if you try to maneuver around the situation and take the first turn out of there, you're only going to be faced with the lesson again down the road.

Life is meant to teach you. Learn from mistakes, repeat the processes that render positive outcomes, and grow from your challenges. If times are tough right now then grab a pen and paper, and let's get studying! Time to nail this test!

Knowing that life is all about a journey of ups and downs, we need to be aware of all the side roads and slip our internal alarm system into 4x4 when we know we're headed for a bumpy ride.

There's no use in always taking the easy path when that won't teach us anything about the hills of life. Embrace the next time you recognize, *I've gone through this before!* And think to yourself, *What was my passing grade the last time? Oh, I failed. This time, I'm prepared to learn so I can apply the outcome again in the future.*

So if you're presented with a consistent situation at work or in your relationships, maybe it's time to wonder if there's learning and growth to be had from taking the test. If you do all the work to educate yourself on what you're faced with, chances are you'll come out a better person, with a heightened appreciation and understanding for the people and situations on your journey. Maybe it's something about your character you need to learn. Maybe it's a skill that needs to be developed to take your career to the next level. Maybe it's an emotion that you need to feel, or a thought process you need to break free from. Whatever it is, it's there to serve you. Besides, giving up will only mean you need to go through it again in the future.

So go on, get a study buddy, take some extra courses, read a book, do whatever you got to do—just don't drop out. Think about all the great things you've accomplished so far in your journey, and that this will be another triumph to add to your wall of "hard work pays off."

Go for that A+.

The Usual Suspects

I remember after indulging on a Thanksgiving weekend, I wasn't surprised with how I felt the days after that four-day binge! It's baaaaack ... Yup! That's right, those usual suspects and symptoms came creeping up as I let my lifestyle choices go rampant. Having just switched work locations, stopped exercising regularly (because I left my personal trainer at the old location), my eating habits took a major turn as I spent a week on the road for work, and my sleep varied as I had new and different stressors introduced each day. Following these three weeks of change came Thanksgiving with all my favourite treats! I wasn't caught off guard when my little protective sensations started alerting me, "Warning. You're entering a past zone deemed off limits now. Warning!"

After taking a couple of weeks off my more balanced routine, I surely noticed the difference when it came to anxiety levels. I started to fear driving again and started to think about all the bad things that might happen down the road. I know very well that this is a by-product of being off balance. Having too much processed sugar in my diet creates more anxious sensations, which triggers the old thoughts and the old patterns of behaviours that used to have a very comfortable home in my mind.

Having broken sleep made me more exhausted and vulnerable to stressors.

Not exercising made my body less energized and all those positive endorphins weren't being released as often as they used to be.

And then, I started thinking about my past life with all that anxiety and what would happen if it came back!

It's just like riding a bike … your mind doesn't forget how to think those thoughts! Especially when the patterns were engraved in your thought process for so many years.

Looking back at that time, I didn't really notice how day by day my positive lifestyle was slowly being taken over by the hustle and bustle of my crazy life!

Once I started experiencing those anxious symptoms and negative thought patterns, I knew I had let my protective side take over. It's never too late to make the switch. I knew I would just have to go back to what I always knew worked!

Take a Step Back

Your life is a reflection of your current and past thoughts. That includes all the good and all the undesirable thoughts. It's easy to see what you think about most by looking at your life. Are you happy? Frustrated? Depressed? Unfulfilled? Grateful?

If you look at your life and something isn't feeling right, then you need to be aware that your thoughts are making that feeling a reality for you.

If you're frustrated, then the thoughts you are and have been thinking will lead back to all things frustrating. You've probably been over thinking events or situations that frustrate you. The law of attraction keeps sending more people, events, or circumstances that'll continue to frustrate you.

It can be challenging to have gratitude or patience for your journey when you're surrounded by people who are farther along than you. You need to be aware that they too started at the beginning of their journey at some point. Perhaps they started two years ago or two weeks ago. Whatever it may be, you can't measure your personal successes or challenges based on where someone else is or has been. Be on your own path and make the decisions that are right for you. You never know what may be going on behind the scenes of a journey that is not yours.

When you really dig into it, most often you wouldn't want what another person has. The image of certain lifestyles can be deceiving … just do *you*.

When you feel like your current life is not on track with your ultimate "happy place," take a minute and step outside to an objective point of view. Look back and consider what you've been thinking lately. Are your thoughts on the same frequency as your current feelings and reality? Ah-ha! You just realized how it works, eh?

Mind Fitness Challenge:

Each time you feel a negative feeling, physically take an actual step back and recall your most common recent thoughts. Do they match? If so, think a more positive thought, something that would be on the frequency of what you actually want. Even if you don't have what you want in this moment, just think it.

Then take a step forward and continue to think thoughts along the positive frequency. Be aware each time those negative thoughts reappear and take an actual step back, change the thought to what you want that's positive, and step forward again. Repeat.

You'll notice that each time you do this you're changing your pattern of thinking. By pairing your mental thought with using the physical movement of taking a step back, you're training your brain to bridge a connection between your mind and body.

Soon enough it'll become a habit and you can consciously change your thoughts quicker and catch them before they become your reality!

Chapter 5

Your Mess Is Your Message

That Silver Lining

In 2012 I decided to start a blog website to journal about my recovery process. I called it My Mind Fitness.

I recorded all my ah-ha moments, my perils, my wisdom, and my life changing discoveries.

A spark inside me said that I would do BIG things with this in the future. I would grow this as a movement. I had known firsthand that those who suffered with physical health ailments could seek support and guidance through so many positive avenues (like the fitness club I worked at), yet those who battled a journey with mental health were basically on their own.

I knew this struggle would become my greatest gift to offer the world. I understood at this point how every incident of your life becomes the story of your success.

What seemed to be such a mess that I was living, would ultimately be the message that I would spend the rest of my life preaching about. I knew in the depths of my soul this was true.

And so I kept blogging.

I also contacted a lawyer to start what would be a two-year process to trademark the name Mind Fitness (in Canada).

I was guided in this direction to start a movement towards creating a space of positive power around achieving mental wellness, just as I helped people do every day with their physical health.

I will never forget the day when I was driving to work, sun beaming through the windshield of my car and I literally heard God call on me. I felt peace with my struggles and the hardships I had been enduring. I knew I had been put on this Earth for a purpose. That flash of intuition and guidance stuck with me for all challenging and trying days ahead. It was clear I had a bigger calling. I knew I was meant for so much more than to be just a girl with anxiety.

Even though I still had a lot of life to experience before it would unfold for me, I knew in my heart I was meant to walk this path.

Look How Far You've Come

Often times we look at our journey and feel as though it's never going to end. Sorry to break the news, but it won't. Your journey is your life. It will be active and progressing for as long as you're breathing. There are some ways you can exercise your mind so that this ride you're on is one you can be proud of and feel accomplished about.

A mind fitness journey is very similar to a weight loss journey. The unit of measurement may be different, but the concept is still the same. It is important to look at how far you've come and give yourself some credit for the amazing steps you have taken to get this far. Whether you have just taken your very first step or you're a mile down the road, look back and smile. See the past behind you as all the lessons, courage, and bravery that have brought you to be who you are today.

I look at my own journey this way. More than a decade ago I started with my anxiety at a 10/10. It completely took over my life. I had no way out, no hope, and was grabbing at anything I thought could "fix" me. Let's use a common parallel of weight loss.

It's as if I started my journey needing to lose 100 pounds. After consistent dedication and effort, I lost an amazing 80 pounds! Yes, I still had 20 pounds to go, but I had to be proud of what I had shed so far. It's not easy to lose 80 pounds and it's even harder to keep it off. The most crucial and long-lasting part of any journey is focusing on the successes that have brought you to where you are now, and continuing to find what works for the rest of the distance you have to go. If the case is that I never lose that last 20 pounds, do I give myself permission to be okay with that? A big change is finding that self-love that says, "I'm perfect just the way I am." If I lose that 20 pounds or not, I'm perfect being me. If having that extra 20 pounds is not bringing you peace and you feel as though you're not living to your full potential, keep going to shed the last bit!

Everyone's journey is unique.

The truth is, I may forever live with a little piece of me that needs to be accommodated in situations that previously caused me full-blown panic attacks. I will still do everything in life but with a little twist so I'm comfortable.

I remember thinking how I didn't ask the Universe to send me this condition. I didn't ask to create these thought patterns and behavioural tendencies. Regardless of my intentions, there was a reason why my journey went in this direction. I can now see clearly how all the pain I suffered in these years had led me to the door to my spirit, a side of me I had never really met. I can't thank this journey enough for providing me with that insight.

I now know that I can handle anything life throws at me, because I've had years of practice finding out who I am and what I'm made of.

It's imperative that you listen to your mind, body, and emotions. They send you messages and signals for what's off-balance, so you can restore the energy flow.

Look back at your starting point; now look at where you are today. If you've started your journey, you've already lost a couple "pounds." The road is not paved, but the trail you leave behind is full of life's greatest lessons.

Embrace this journey and be proud of yourself for starting it. Know that every healer in this life came from being a wounded person. So as you start to mend yourself, you will become the source of healing for others.

Now get back out there and continue walking; your path awaits you.

What Gift Do You Get?

What gift does your challenge give you? For me, I had always looked at my anxiety as a challenge and hateful habit of behaviours, when in actuality, there was a positive lesson to be learned.

Throughout the years there were times I was forced to take a step back, but other times when I was also able to experience each moment and memory to its fullest because I put so much thought and effort into making it comfortable. Seeing how far I came throughout the journey would make me realize that when I did resort to avoidance (avoiding situations or events that would typically trigger anxious sensations), I was typically off-balance.

I have such sensitive internal alarms that go off to alert me when I need to check in to see if I'm neglecting my mind, body, or spirit, even to this day.

After years of learning about alternative healing, I have a catalogue of resources to reference that will get me back on track. Sometimes I need to get another Thai massage to open my meridian lines. Other times, I need to increase my workouts, or take some time to meditate and reflect. Without the personal need and motivation to better my life from my undesired behaviours, I would never have stumbled upon all the amazing modalities I've now studied and become certified in.

Through these experiences I can now assist other individuals facing similar challenges, or starting their own journeys. If I had not gone through my journey, I wouldn't have been able to share it with you today.

So think about what positive gifts your challenge has given you. Let me teach you something I learned in my certification for Neuro-Linguistic Programming (studying the language of the mind). When we have undesired behaviours, it's because there is a secondary benefit from them, or a "positive intention" that our subconscious mind is working hard at to keep us safe, comfortable, and free from harm.

It's important that we find our "positive intention" in our undesired behaviours and really place true meaning on our journey. The only way we'll be able to break free from the mental ropes that keep us tied down, is to acknowledge the benefit that comes from not letting go of those actions. All of our undesired behaviours have a secondary benefit to us, which is why we keep doing them. For me what triggered my anxiety was often linked to the need to be in control. By keeping up that "anxiety girl" identity, I could continue to control all situations I was in.

Once I acknowledged why I was behaving a certain way, I began to challenge myself to give up control and let other people make decisions. The more I gave up control, the more I learned that it's okay to surrender.

Mind Fitness Challenge:

Go somewhere quiet where you can't be disturbed. If possible, turn on meditation or calming music. If it suits you better, just sit in complete silence. Close your eyes. Take a series of deep breaths until you find yourself in total relaxation. Ask your subconscious mind why it chooses to protect you with the undesired behaviour you keep repeating. Ask yourself why you continue this habit or behaviour. What's the purpose? More often than not, you'll be able to tap into your true intentions. By allowing your body to be in a state of relaxation, you give your spirit and emotions a chance to connect with your mind.

You'll be placing a heightened focus on finding your meaning. Now you can move towards new actions that still satisfy your "positive intention" without having to resort to those undesired behaviours.

Chapter 6

When It ALL Finally Made Sense

The Moment It All Pieced Together

Up to this point you've been led to believe my anxiety started in 2002 when I started university. Not that I'm trying to mislead you, but until that point, I didn't know any better myself.

Until a Reiki (energy healing) session I had in the spring of 2013.

In an effort to create a sense of balance to my mind and body, I went through a couple months where I consistently scheduled these incredibly relaxing reiki treatments on my lunch break at work. But there was one particular day that opened the biggest door yet for my healing.

I was deep in mediation, to the point that I had fallen asleep on the massage table. The lights were off, the room lit only by a salt lamp in the corner and the gas fireplace. The music was calming and all I could feel was the powerful energy flow through the hands of my healer and warm my entire body.

All of a sudden I had this vivid flashback of when I was four years old, almost as if I was dreaming. I sat up from the table and looked at my practitioner (who's like a second mom to me), and with a shaky voice let out, "I know why I've suffered from this bathroom phobia for all these years! It all makes sense!"

Clearly confused, she asked me to elaborate.

This childhood memory was so clear—like it was just yesterday.

I remembered my cute blue dress, white leotards and little white shoes with embroidered yellow flowers on them. I remembered my bus buddy, Michelle, who sat beside me on the way home from junior kindergarten.

I had to go pee so badly. I stood up and asked Sandy, the bus driver, to stop so I could go to the bathroom.

I remember her looking up in the oversized review mirror and with a stern gaze she yelled at me, "SIT DOWN! DO NOT stand up on a moving bus!!"

I had no choice. I had to go pee.

I looked at Michelle beside me and asked her if she wanted to see a magic trick. I told her I could turn my shoes into sprinklers. And then I did it. I peed my pants (well, dress).

On our way off the bus, Sandy yelled at me again and all the boys laughed in the front seats as I exited.

My friend's mom, Maggie, was waiting for us to get off the bus and Sandy gave her an earful about how I needed to learn to use the bathroom before I get on her bus again and how now she had to work late to clean it up.

I felt embarrassed, ashamed, and ridiculed.

I was traumatized.

Maggie gave me a bath when we got home and some of my friend's clothes.

Until this day, my mom still doesn't recall this ever happening, but I do.

I mean, to my mom I was a four year old who had an accident, but for me, I would never forget the shame and embarrassment I felt that day.

For the rest of that school year, I hid behind my cubby if I ever had to go pee. My teachers would ask me why I was hiding and I would reply, "I have to go to the bathroom and what if you say no?"

It was remembering this moment that made sense of everything for me.

Looking at the last 23 years of my life, I started connecting the dots.

I now understood why as a young girl I'd make sure I knew where every bathroom was before sitting down in a restaurant or at a new person's house. My parents always made fun of me for it, not understanding my obsession with bathrooms. Click! Now that made sense.

Going off to university, I was in my first living situation where I was sharing a washroom with 15 other girls. Now I understood why my social embarrassment came back full circle. What *if* they made fun of me for needing to go to the bathroom? Sounds ridiculous, but it was my reality.

I then also realized that on the day of my very first panic attack (the stoplight trauma), I must have had a flashback of being stuck in a moving vehicle, needing to go to the bathroom, and being told in a stern angry voice, "JUST WAIT!"

My whole life was centred around that one traumatic event when I was four years old.

Here's where the magic lies. Once you recognize and can be honest with yourself and your traumas, you begin to really heal.

I knew damn well I was hiding that moment in captivity for the better part of my life in my subconscious mind.

Remember when I told you that years ago my therapist asked me, "Do you have *any* reason to believe you will not make it to a bathroom in time? Has it ever happened to you where you *did not* make it in time and that embarrassed you and that's what has caused this fear?" And every time I responded no; I had such resistance. Well, that was because I knew it was a lie.

This little voice inside me would try yelling, "YES! When I was four I peed my pants on the school bus and everyone laughed at me." But, crazy enough, I was an adult and too embarrassed to admit it.

I couldn't help but think to myself, *What if I had been honest to that therapist when I was first diagnosed with this panic disorder? What would have all these years of my life looked like instead?*

But, there's a reason for every decision we make. And we have to just have faith that it all lines up as it should.

So, what did I do the day this memory bubbled up to the surface and I finally gave it life outside of my mind?

Well, I decided to let the skeletons out of the closet...

I went back to work and I admitted to a few of my co-workers about the memory I had just unlocked from the depths of my soul.

And, as any normal group of girls would do ... they laughed. A lot. And so did I. Then they went on to tell me about the last time they peed or pooped their pants. And to my surprise, all of them had an experience within the last YEAR!

So we told stories of not making it to a bathroom in time for our whole meeting–laughing and bringing light to what, for me, was the darkest secret I had ever kept. It sounds so silly, because what kid doesn't pee their pants? But to me it was a pivotal moment of shame I experienced in my young life, so I did everything to protect myself from ever feeling that way again. After allowing myself to be open about it, I finally released the fear and shame and allowed in the truth. The truth being, there was NOTHING to be ashamed of.

Well, that little nugget could have saved me a lifetime of traumatic stress.

But then, I wouldn't be here to share my story, would I?

Hindsight is Always 20/20

They say hindsight is 20/20. So what does that even mean?

The way I look at it is that once you become fully aware of a situation or experience you've just overcome, you may look back and realize how differently you would have done things if you only knew how it was going to work out in the end.

A couple years ago I watched a video of Steve Jobs giving a speech to a graduating class at Stanford University. There was one quote from that video that stuck with me: "You can't connect the dots looking forward; you can only connect the dots looking backwards. So you have to trust the dots will somehow connect in your future. You have to trust in something — your gut, destiny, life, karma, whatever. This approach has never let me down, and it has made all the difference in my life."

In essence, you can't predict what your future holds, how your experiences or your journey will unfold, or foreshadow the consequences of your choices. Why? Because you don't know what you don't know. It's not until you have those ah-ha moments that things start to make sense. Then you look back and wish it could've been different. But here's the thing—you could never have connected those dots looking forward, so don't beat yourself up over it.

Once you do know, then you can make the right choices, take responsibility and accountability for your part, and move forward. This might mean moving forward in a different direction. The most important thing is to live life knowing that every choice you make is with positive intention. If you know that you've walked each step in your journey with the intention that serves you and those around you with love and respect, then looking back you'll know that you acted in good faith. If some things didn't unfold the way you hoped for, now that you know what you know, then that's part of your journey and now is the time to make some changes. The only constant thing in life is change. So embrace it.

A lot of people ask me, "Well how do I get over what this person did to me? If I had known this is how it would have ended up I would never have gotten involved in the first place!" But you didn't know what you didn't know. Now, it is what it is. Are you catching on?

So here's my advice. Never hate another person for their actions. It doesn't mean they are bad people; they just may have acted in bad behaviour. So forgive them (not necessarily to their face, but inside you, forgive them) and let them live out the consequences of their own behaviour so you can move on.

For some people it may look like this, "I don't dislike you and I'll never resent or speak poorly about you. Those are negative emotions I don't need to carry with me in my life. Those emotions can only bring me down. However, for what you've done there are consequences, and the consequence is that you'll never have me in your life again." You can only take care of you and what is within your control. It's a powerful thing to let go, move on, and let someone else deal with the consequences of their own behaviour without you.

It's the same message for getting over the pain you've endured on your mental health journey. Once you become aware of what isn't working for you, you can change it. You can seek support, get the right tools, read books like this one (humble brag), and make the changes.

Once you know what you know, you have to make choices. This could be in relationships, careers, or personal choices. As long as in your journey you live with positive intention for all that you do, you can't look back with regret. Forgive those who have wronged you, and let them live with the consequences of their behaviour. Don't carry that around in your spirit or mind.

Forgive yourself for perhaps not stepping up for your health earlier.

All these experiences are there to shape and make you. Your journey is about creating a life through the lessons you learn from what your experiences have taught you.

Hindsight may be 20/20, but I'd rather squint looking forward than live a life reading the ending first.

The Dreaded GGOTOSS (Go-tis)

What is GGOTOSS you might be asking? It's the dreaded Grass is Greener On The Other Side Syndrome. This can strike just about anyone who isn't satisfied with "enough". I termed GGOTOSS back when I gave a speech to the top 500 associates in our company when I worked in the fitness industry.

I typically hear people in our generation talking about how another job would be more fun or less stress. How if they had a bigger house they'd be happier; if they had a better partner they would have their needs met.

It always seems that enough is never good enough. When in reality, if you got those things, you would eventually find faults in them too.

If we let ourselves constantly think about what we don't have, instead of being grateful for what we do have, we'll never find joy in our lives. Here's the brutal reality—someone will *always* have more money than you, a better house than you, a nicer car than you, a better looking partner than you, a less stressful job than you, or a seemingly better lifestyle than you. That being said, you don't know their story.

You don't know what they go through every day to have that. You don't know if they feel any peace or joy in their lives because *things* and joy don't go hand in hand.

Try looking at it this way—the grass is greener where you water it. When something is fresh, exciting, and new, you're dousing water (positive energy) onto your grass. You're still enjoying it so you see all the great things about it, whether it's a new job, a new relationship, a new car, etc. After the honeymoon stage wears off you stop watering it as much. You're not as excited anymore so you forget to nurture it like you used to. Soon you start to notice the weeds as they grow and multiply and start consuming your once-perfect green lawn.

Instead of recognizing that your once-perfect lawn is no more and go back to fertilizing it and nurturing it, you decide to move. Find a new, fresh lawn where you can start again. You can spend your whole life packing up and moving, or you can be grateful for what you have and keep watering your own lawn.

Nurture it and keep it green. When the time is right, you can expand your lawn into acres of fresh green luscious grass, building on top of the greatness you've kept going all these years. The last thing you want is to look back and realize that all your dreams have actually come true, but instead of letting them happen in due time, you rushed to the next step and didn't get to enjoy the ride because you always felt behind on your journey.

Let life take you at its own pace. Let there be peace in knowing that the dreams will come no matter what, so enjoy the process! All the hiccups are lessons you need to learn; don't shrug them off or try to find something better—just embrace where you are, whether you feel it's the best place right now or not. There's a reason for everything!

Before I recognized where my trauma had stemmed from (so I could heal from it), I was constantly trying to change my environment, change my circumstances, change anything I could easily give up. The hope was that life would be easier on the other side of those things. That being said, no matter where I went or where I ended up, my problems still followed me. They were inside of me. They were part of me, waiting to be healed.

I had to stop looking at all the reasons why things were wrong, and I had to start looking for all the things that were going right.

Let's refer back to when I talked about looking at how far you've come. It's important to be grateful for the process, the progress, and the possibilities in front of us.

Mind Fitness Challenge:

Every day, wake up and tell yourself everything you're grateful for. Water your grass with positive energy and thankfulness! Train your mind to look for the positive and how to recognize that you're in the right place. Check in with yourself next week and see if you notice a difference in appreciation for the wonderful life you have!

Chapter 7

A New Chapter

Making the Change

I wish I could say that after forgiving Sandy, the bus driver, for scolding me as a child, all my problems went away.

However, I still had some work to do.

I had spent my whole life up until this point creating protective mental barriers, so it was naturally going to take some time to rewire my brain, even after I learned to exercise forgiveness.

The change wasn't just about introducing positive mental habits. The major hindrance to my full recovery was the fact that I was still engaging in lifestyle choices that kept my body in a state of exhaustion (like drinking heavily on weekends, having copious amounts of coffee each day, and over working). As far as I had come with my recovery, I had hit a point where it was all or nothing.

In the summer of 2014, I was faced with a time in my career as a general manager where I could no longer keep up with the long hours, sales pressure, and demand for perfection that I put on myself. I knew that to take my recovery to the next level I had to let go of my status, title, great pay cheques, and the need to be the best in the company.

I'd hit another point where the Universe had made it so uncomfortable for me to stay doing what I was doing, that it forced me to make a decision.

On August 26, 2014, I sat patiently in my doctor's office awaiting test results. I took the day off to investigate why I started getting shakes in my hands and why my heart beat felt irregular. My doctor came into the room and said to me, "Jennifer, I highly encourage you to take a month off work. Otherwise, next time you're sitting here it will be much worse." I had started shaking so badly because my adrenal glands were over worked, I was constantly tired, and my body was taxed. To me, it felt like I was waving the white flag. My poor body had gone through so much over the years and just couldn't take any more stress or damage, and I wasn't interested in wasting anymore time not feeling my absolute best.

I was aware that as much as I had made massive strides for the better with my holistic approaches, I still had parts of my lifestyle that were keeping me unbalanced. My job was the biggest one. I spent 80% of my time in an environment that was action packed, over stimulating, loud, demanding, and controlling.

So, with a trembling hand and nervous as hell, I handed in a two-week medical leave of absence to my boss the next morning (I negotiated with my doctor from one month to two weeks).

This was actually the first time in my nine-year career that I had ever taken time off for mental wellness.

In those two weeks I became really silent. I became still. I sought counsel and reread a lot of the material I had studied over the last few years. I woke up to no alarm clock, I rested my body; I just did me. It was at that point I made a big decision that changed the trajectory of my journey.

I decided it was time to let go of the career I had worked almost a decade to build. I never thought I would leave my role as general manger unless it was to move *up* in the company, but I needed to do what was best for me.

I thought I would spend so much time mourning my old career, but honestly, I felt so EXHILARATED!

I took a new position with our head office in Human Resources so I could work fewer hours, with less pressure and a less stimulating environment. I knew it would just be temporary while I figured out what I was going to do with my life now, and it was the perfect position to let me take a breather.

I also decided at this point that I would turn My Mind Fitness (remember that blog website I started back in 2012?) into a full coaching practice.

I wanted to help guide others who I saw as a former version of myself. People who had hit rock bottom, felt stuck in their circumstances with no way out, people struggling to find mental freedom. I had just busted through those doors and was ready to help guide others, on top of all the amazing tools I had learned along the way!

I knew this would be part of my life's purpose, and now with this new work-life balance, I would have the time and peace to open up new opportunities that were aligned with my purpose.

This career move was the beginning of my new life.

Turn the Page

Consider your life a book series. Each book of your life has a different ending. The only thing that stays constant is you; you are the main character. By the end of your life you will have a shelf of books, representing the series of your life. Each book has a different plot, has some characters that don't make an appearance in the next book, and has different adventures. When we look at our library we will see that some of the books of our lives are romantic comedies, thrillers, suspense, drama or tragedy, and some could have been a fairy tale. It's important to learn how to embrace the different genres and how to appreciate when some situations in our lives come to an end, because that means there is a brand new beginning about to happen! I learned this lesson a couple years ago after trying to understand why I was feeling so down and unfulfilled after an amazing couple of years.

Let me explain. After playing "the waiting game" with Dave, he finally proposed. I was so excited! I got to spend the next year and a half planning my dream wedding. In the year leading up to the wedding, I had two bridal showers, a stag and doe, a bachelorette party, a week-long destination wedding, a wedding reception at home two months later, and an amazing honeymoon in Jamaica. This was immediately followed up by renovating our first home, selling it, buying a new beautiful home, moving in, and furnishing it.

Soon afterwards, we planned a wonderful housewarming party with family and friends, and a week later I had a trip to Vegas for my 30th birthday!

The fun was never ending. The "all about me" was still living on!

In the weeks following the last party, I started to realize that things were changing. There were no more events, no big things to look forward to.

Now what?

Then a traumatic moment happened: our little fur baby of 16 years (our cat, Kaylee) fell terminally ill, and within hours of finding out, we had to make a quick decision to send her to kitty heaven. I felt like I had nothing left. I felt like I had hit a wall. I didn't know what would make me happy anymore. Everything had changed; I was not used to a quiet house, not to mention no more parties and "to-dos" all about me.

Then I realized this is life. All I had really done was finished the last chapter and turned the last page of another book in my series. I was now able to put that book up on the shelf with the rest of them. Now, I got to open a new book, with new stories, new challenges, new joys, new experiences, and new people.

When I look at the main character now, I see there are two. I share my life equally in this new book with my husband, and our relationship is different from the last book.

It's important that we recognize when one of our books has ended. If we keep re-reading a current or past chapter, or don't have the courage to close a book when it has ended, then we can never start a new one. So, if you're ready for a new start, a new beginning, then it's okay to turn that last page.

Put that book on the shelf and leave it there. There's no point going back to read the past hoping to find answers or wonder why the book turned out the way it did. It's already written, so let it be. It brought you to the next one.

Opening the front cover of the next book in your series is exciting. Once you become aware of this power, you can start to choose the genre your next book is going to be and start to write the text based on what you want to have in your life.

So how about it? Why don't you go ahead and turn that page?

The End.

Mind Your Feathers

I have recently become very aware of a pattern of behaviour that people (including myself!) exercise in life when in certain situations. This pattern is not very useful or sustainable long term, and for that reason I wanted to become more conscious of when I was doing it so I could choose the right path.

What I'm talking about is "peacocking."

Peacocking is what I refer to when you're in a situation where you flaunt your feathers for attention. "Hey look at me! I'm beautiful and amazing at this and that. I'm fun, gracious, generous, and appreciative. I can accomplish anything and can take on any task. I own x, y, z. I'm the total package. I'm the perfect person for you to choose as an employee, partner, friend". (You get the drift.)

As you may know, when male peacocks are trying to get the attention of a mate, they display their beautiful feathers as an attraction technique.

Here's the downfall: after the chase is over, or once you've landed what you were attracting, you let your feathers back down and the real authentic you is what's left. If you're not internally happy with that person, then you may find yourself constantly needing people or situations that allow you to peacock. This can lead to GGOTOSS and a constant need for something or someone new.

If we love who we are when peacocking and find ourselves empty when not, then naturally, we assume the best solution is live in that state of attention. I'm going to tell you why it's actually not in your best interest to do so.

As mentioned, you only allow yourself to exhibit certain behaviours when peacocking (characteristics that make you desirable), which, in turn, gives you loads of attention. You, of course, love getting the attention, so you always find yourself looking for new ways to display your feathers. This may mean changing your job position, materialistic goods, your partner, or social circle. It may lead to you constantly changing your surroundings so you have new people or places to attract.

Once people know the real you, because let's face it, you can't always be fabulous and "on," you feel the need to search out someone or something new that will find your initial energy irresistible again.

This pattern is typically a result of an inner spiritual imbalance. It's part of our approval-seeking behaviour. There are parts of your authentic character that you're not at peace with and would rather not live with.

So, instead of living in a state of "it's *show time!*" how about we work on *you*? Work on finding out who you really are and finding peace and joy with what's inside. Anyone who knows me knows I love to

70

peacock. I love to be "on" and live in that moment and excitement of meeting new people, and embark on new journeys. And that is perfectly normal! It's a basic human instinct.

That being said, a lot about my authentic self also has similar characteristics to what I display when I'm flaunting, so I have a hard time knowing when to let down my feathers or how to distinguish between the two.

One of my greatest resources is my husband, who can remind me of all the reasons why he loves the real me. Authentic, down to earth, unconditionally loved, and yes, flawed, me.

Do you have someone in your life who can point out all the amazing qualities of the <u>real</u> you?

Be conscious of only surrounding yourself with situations that make you flaunt your feathers. At some point, you'll need to put them down and you don't want an emotional crash. Peacocking can be an extremely addictive behaviour. The high that the attention gives you can be irresistible to your neurology and physiology.

Just being aware of when you are doing it can help you mind your feathers and bring them down in due time.

Take it from me, it is absolutely fun to flaunt all the great qualities and potential you have. However, getting into a cycle of constantly seeking out new situations to peacock in can be destructive to your life, and result in feelings of dissatisfaction and ungratefulness with those things that may not be so new (basically those things you've already landed).

Nothing will seem as exciting in your life if you can't find happiness with what you already have when your beautiful display of feathers aren't showing.

So instead of looking for other people, events, or situations that allow you to flair your goods and get attention, go find all the amazing things that you love about you within yourself. No feathers, just plain old you.

Learn to enjoy your own company. Love your strengths and own your weaknesses. Learn to detach your happiness from people or things, as their actions and reactions can directly influence your thoughts and feelings. The more you fall in love with the authentic you (not your ego), the less you will crave the high from the addictive behaviours and ultimately the less you will need to live in "peacock mode" as it can be exhausting.

It may also be useful to notice when someone else may be in "peacock mode" too, so you don't get caught up in the infatuation of it all. Always keep your eyes and heart open to seeing someone for who they really are, whatever about them is desirable or undesirable, and just love them unconditionally. This will help remove the blinders that fog our true vision.

Once again, peacocking is totally natural and a basic human/animal instinct, but it's not meant to be abused. Just as our bodies are naturally equipped to fight-or-flight when faced with danger, we aren't meant to live in a constant state of anxiety about situations that really pose no threat to us.

Start to notice if you find yourself living in that attention-seeking state more often than not, and use that as your alarm code for restoring the balance with your spirit.

If you feel this has been you, I think it's time to go rest those tired feathers.

You Are a Product of Your Environment

Take a look around you. What kind of people or situations do you surround yourself with? Most people who are aware that they need to make a change, will start to see a reflection of their environment in their struggles to keep a fit and healthy mind.

If you spend eight hours a day in an unhealthy work environment, and then take that energy home with you, it can make for an unpleasant life. What do I mean by unhealthy environment? It can be as simple as being surrounded by coworkers who gossip, are unhappy with their job, constantly talk poorly about the company/their position, and the list goes on.

Soon enough you get in on the dirt too. In order to feel like you're on the same frequency as the rest of the culture you become a clone of those attitudes. This can be especially troubling for someone looking to make positive lifestyle changes to improve their mind fitness.

The same goes for if your friends are the type that always gossip about the friend who isn't there. To feel like you fit in, or simply to be part of the conversation, you mould into that behaviour and start contributing your opinions. Of course, what ends up happening when you leave? You wonder what everyone is saying about *you* now that you're not there. Or worse, are they telling the poor friend who wasn't present your opinions of them? It's a vicious cycle.

Think of other people as outlets. When you plug into them they will either charge you or drain your battery.

So what do you do? The first step is recognizing that you don't feel all warm and fuzzy inside when you're in these environments. If you don't find anything wrong with this way of living, then you don't believe you need a change. If you do find it troublesome to be in the middle of the negative gossip group, here's a challenge to try:

Mind Fitness Challenge:

Every time something negative is said about someone else, be the first to speak up with a positive counter about that individual. It's amazing to see the reaction on people's faces when one person goes against the flow of energy. If the energy in that moment is one of jealously, judgment, or ridicule, and one person tries to inject positivity, you can surely feel the resistance.

Don't let that stop you! Soon enough you will notice how your positive words can bring about more positive healthy thoughts or feelings. Have you ever heard of the law of attraction? It basically states that whatever you put out into the Universe gets sent back to you with more like thoughts or feelings. It's like a magnet—like thoughts attract like thoughts, whether it's negative or positive. Eventually your entire circle of influence will change to match what your predominant thoughts and feelings are, and if that means you get a more positive environment out of it—well then I think it's a very worthwhile challenge!

Chapter 8

A Natural Approach

God's Gifts of the Earth

A few weeks following my decision to leave my coveted corporate career path, I met a girl who introduced me to plant-based medicine for mind mood management. She gifted me a few bottles of essential oils that I could use for shifting my moods and helping with this new job transition. I had these beautifully natural aromas running in my office on the daily, and could immediately feel the difference with my stress levels.

I had never heard of essential oils before, so this was a new avenue for me.

Having taken a holistic and natural approach to my recovery in the previous years, it was right up my alley!

I began to learn a lot about emotional aromatherapy and could see how nature really has provided us with every tool to live an optimal, healthy life. I quickly decided to bring them into my new coaching practice with clients.

Before I knew it I registered myself to become an educator with the essential oils company, dōTERRA (meaning gifts of the earth). Fast forward two years—I ranked as one of the top 7% global leaders for this company. Needless to say, emotional wellness was my niche!

Teaching about pure and potent essential oils and the power behind natural plant therapy has been one of the highlights of my career! Nothing gives me more joy than helping another person who is just starting their journey towards mental health.

Using essential oils for mood management and supporting emotions is so simple, effective, and best of all, has nothing but positive side effects.

Embarking on this chapter of my life, I feel, was the last piece of the puzzle. I was able to support my body as I got off the rest of my medication and over-the-counter tummy tamers. I was also surrounded by a community that was well versed in natural approached to wellness, which contributed to the consistency of my positive habits and choices.

The Greatest Lifestyle Change Goes To ...

On January 28th, 2015, right after I was introduced to essential oils, I decided to take the last leap into my recovery.

My FUEL.

My nutrition.

I committed to a four-month full reparative digestive overhaul with a clinical holistic nutritionist.

During these four months, I went on a social media detox (absolutely NO social media!), no alcohol, no coffee, nothing but the right fuel to repair my leaky gut and re-create the connection from my brain to my second brain—the gut.

We used a protocol that establishes a connection between the functions of the digestive system and the brain. Repair your gut health = repair your mental health. With most of your body's serotonin (your happy chemical) produced in your gut, and many other key hormones and chemicals associated with optimal mental health being impacted by a healthy gut environment, it was imperative we started here.

Did you know there's a nerve that runs from your stomach to your brain? Yeah, neither did I! It makes so much sense why you have a gut instinct and why you are what you eat.

I drank bone broth for five weeks straight, cooked all my own food, pre-packed all my lunches, and never ate out (being on a strict diet will limit a lot of options).

Throughout this process I learned to connect with my body like I never had before. I gained a new respect and compassion for what our bodies *do for* us but also what they *need from* us.

At the end of those four months, my husband and I ended up pregnant!

I knew my body was in the best health it had ever been.

I was now completely off of all medication.

I was cutting out all toxic load in my home (I'll be going deeper into this later) by using my essential oils to make all of my products. I was resting properly, managing my stress, and was finally feeling like I had meaning and purpose in life.

I was even more motivated to stay healthy, so I could give my baby the best vessel to grow in.

And I did just that.

I kept pouring into my health and wellness, learning more and more about what we put in our bodies through our food, environment and body care products, and how to do the best I can do to make natural, healthy choices.

Throughout my daughter's little life, I have continued to pass my knowledge onto how I fuel her body too.

When you know better you do better, right?

Feeding Your Mind, Body, and Soul

How simple is it to be the healthiest you?

Very basic.

How easy is it to execute these basic practices?

Very challenging.

It takes so much dedication and power to make positive changes, but let me tell you that the rewards are incredibly evident and worth it. When I first started my journey, almost every practitioner taught me the same principles. I didn't want to believe them; I wanted to believe there was an easier, quicker fix to my problems. That's why I kept going to different people for different opinions. When in actuality, the most cost-effective and time-effective answers all lay in the same place—within *me*.

So here is the simplest, most basic way of outlining where your journey should start ...

Feed Your MIND
Exercising the mind is the same as the body. It requires roughly a half hour per day to see dramatic differences.

Feed your mind with positive thoughts, certain behaviours, and surround yourself with an environment that allows for the right type of mental stimulation. Removing negative influences (whether it be people, social media, news, loud places, etc.) can go a long way. Reading educational or self-development books and going to self-development seminars keep the mind positively active.

Past traumatic events can cause our brains to make connections that'll trigger similar events in the future, and this is where we start to see a pattern emerge.

Let's use my example of my bathroom phobia. Everywhere I went after my "stoplight trauma," I had an anxiety or panic attack because of the connection my brain made to that certain incident. My subconscious mind was doing its job in sending off alarms anytime it felt threatened when we didn't have immediate access to a bathroom. Remember how we talked about the positive intention? The intention was to keep me safe, which is wonderful. However the behaviour of anxiety, demanding constant control of my surroundings etc., became the outcome, which I obviously didn't enjoy experiencing.

So, you need to retrain your brain and remove the negative thought process around certain events to clear the mind of fear. I highly recommend practices like hypnotherapy (rewires subconscious belief patterns), NLP (neuro-linguistic programming), and CBT (cognitive behavioural therapy), to name a few. Sometimes doing these techniques alone won't take you across the finish line; it takes a blend of powerful tools merged together to create a holistic (taking into account the whole you) approach to gaining a more fit & healthy mind.

Feed Your BODY

Another key to starting a successful mind fitness journey is nourishing your body with the right types of food, and fuelling it with loads of water. Your body is a fine-tuned machine that requires oil and gasoline. When you deplete it of the above, it starts to squeak and will eventually break down.

Most of the time it's not what we put *in* our body it's what we *don't* put in it. We have such a lack of nutrients in our soils and food these days that it makes it very hard to get all the vitamins and minerals our bodies need to grow and operate efficiently.

My best advice—seek out a holistic nutritionist who can identify where and what your body is lacking to help heal you through food.

Feed your SOUL

Your spirit and soul need so much TLC in the busy and hectic lives we lead in this day and age. Make sure you're taking time every day to meditate or to sit quietly where you feel comfortable in a place that offers you peace and quiet. Connect with the earth, feel the warm breeze on your skin, and just be in the moment.

Try energy healing practices (reiki is an excellent way to get connected and open your chakras) or practice a form of faith. Choose your outlet, but stay connected to your soul. Your soul is the only thing that came with you into this world and will be the only thing that continues on after your body's time is up. So make sure you have a strong affiliation with the authentic you.

There is such an importance to connecting with the earth and unplugging from the noise that has become all too powerful in our environment these days. One of the best challenges I ever took was during my six-week meditation course. I vowed to cut out all TV and social media for two full weeks. Oh, and no radio in the car.

This assignment was the most gratifying of them all. To have the ability to sit in peace on my way to and from work was magical. It was glorious not being over stimulated with news and my friend's amazing social media posts (of course, you only ever get to see the good stuff that makes you envious).

I invite you to disconnect for two weeks. Unplug.

Then you decide if it was the best decision you could have made to help you start your journey.

Starve Your EGO
Our ego can typically lead us down the road of materialism, consumption, and over indulgence. Our ego needs us to feed it, but it's in your best interest to let it starve when it's getting out of control. When you let your ego's power take over, you often lose sight of who you are and who you authentically want to be.

So, if you can swallow this information and accept that this is what it takes, the journey becomes a little easier and a little less complicated.

Your goal is to bring yourself back to a time in this world where life was very basic. Eat to nourish and fuel your body. Connect with your soul to maintain a level of self-awareness and gratitude, and remove the fear of the future, the worry of the past. Be in the moment.

Note: The great thing is being able to be fully aware of your usual suspects—remember when we talked about those earlier? As soon as they start to peek their heads around the corner you need to deny entry. Take a look around you and figure out which door to undesired habits you opened. Was it the bad nutrition? Missing good night's rest? The physical exercise? Have you spent any alone time to reconnect with yourself lately? The wisdom is knowing the difference between allowing yourself a little flexibility with your new positive lifestyle changes and when they are slipping all together.

Mind Fitness Challenge:

Each day for the next seven days write down what you do for yourself to make positive lifestyle changes in each area: mind, body, and spirit. This will be a good opportunity to see what you may be lacking and where you can add some new routines. If you're already doing something for yourself each day in each area—congratulations! That's a huge challenge for most people and this is where we ultimately want to get ourselves. It's much easier to notice what holds us back from living a carefree life when we can pinpoint where/when the balance is off.

What to look for:

Mind: Self-development, positive thinking, expressing love and gratitude, eliminating excessive stimulus (news, social media, etc.).

Body: Exercising, eating three proper, balanced meals a day and mini snacks, taking supplements for added nutrients, limiting or eliminating caffeine and alcohol, staying hydrated, etc.

Spirit: meditating, taking a hot relaxing bath, sitting in nature, praying, etc.

One technique I used when I first started my journey was making a weekly plan which included: my daily meals, my 30-60 minutes of physical exercise, and 30-60 minutes of spiritual connection (usually meditation before bed). I would also make note of catching myself throughout the day if my mind would derail into negative thinking and I would consciously bring it back on track. I did this for 21 days straight to begin to make it a new habit!

So with this Mind Fitness Challenge I want you to just make note of what you're doing "right" already and put in your agenda some new routines you can start!

Then you'll be aware when those usual suspects arrive and you'll know exactly who invited them to the party!

Chapter 9

Your Future Awaits You

Where We Are and Where We Are Going

That brings us to this moment.

It's been four years since my last big lifestyle change (the nutrition overhaul) and I feel amazing.

I'm super connected to knowing what foods will disrupt my moods, I barely drink alcohol, I get a full eight hours of sleep and I am the most balanced and at peace I've ever been.

I haven't had a prescription or pill in almost four years—FOUR YEARS!!

I can't remember my last panic attack, but when I do get anxious, I can usually trace it back to what part of my lifestyle has been a little off.

I still have days or situations that I accommodate for bathrooms, but they're few and far between, and they don't dictate my life.

After more than a decade of triumphs and failures, trying all the "things" and going through the whirlwind of emotions associated with the journey towards optimal mental well-being, I feel I have finally arrived. Arrived at freedom. Arrived at passion and purpose. Arrived at a destination that is only the beginning of a new chapter of my newest book of life.

I truly thought for the rest of my life, I would be just a girl with anxiety and nothing more. I thought it would rule my existence and hinder me from anything fun. I never thought I'd be the mother I wanted to be, or the wife my husband deserved. I'm so glad I was wrong.

Now, to sit here today, writing a book on the truth.

The truth that you have your best life still ahead of you.

Are you ready to open up to the possibilities for what's in store?

It's a Journey for a Reason

Do you think someone got to the point of needing to lose 20 pounds overnight? No. Did you get to the point of having an unhealthy mind overnight? No.

It often takes months to years of repeating undesired habits and thoughts to cause you to be in the position you are today—starting or continuing your journey to a more fit and healthy mind. So remember that it *will* be a challenge at first to retrain your brain and make more positive connections to replace old behaviours or thought patterns. It's just like going to the gym and lifting weights to work on your physical fitness. It takes commitment to start and maintain it. The question just has to be, is it worth it to you to be healthier? Is it worth it to you to change your life? What are the benefits of being anxiety/panic attack free?

Could you imagine your life with less worry and stress about future situations that typically make you fearful? Are you willing to pay the price for the reward of optimal mental health?

The answers to these questions will determine your readiness to start your journey and do the necessary processes to maintain a healthy mind.

One of the things I love about being a Mind Fitness Trainer is that I've been there. I'm still there some days. I know what you're going through and I know what lies ahead. I will likely always be faced with making the choice to do the things that will get me to my ultimate mind fitness goal. It's not easy, but it is simple. Each day I have to make the effort to correct thoughts, eat properly, move, meditate, and do what I need to do to stay balanced (because having a balanced life is essential to recovery).

Even though I've come so far and most days I wonder how I ever went through what I did, I still have to make the right choices everyday if I want to maintain the healthier mind I have now. Don't get me wrong, when I do slip up and feel the consequences of an unbalanced life, I do deal with some anxiety. I just have to pick myself up, look at where I have been, and where I am now, and know that I'm in a better place. We can always start fresh in a minute!

There are days where you'll have hiccups. You'll break and fall into old habits that produce those old results. It doesn't mean you have unlearned all the new behaviours or thought patterns; it just means you need to pause and assess what is off balance so you can adjust.

Remember not to be so hard on yourself when you do make the choice to start the change. It can be a very bumpy road. Be at peace with the small successes and always remember to celebrate them no matter how many hiccups there are. It will take time and practice, but as long as you don't give up on yourself, every day that goes by that you stuck to it is another day closer to your goal.

Every little action step is worth something. Every right choice is a step down the road. Everything you learn along the way will help you, and every obstacle becomes a learning opportunity. Just keep going.

Not everyone makes the choice to change; some believe it's easier to just accept their undesired life as is. You make the right choice for you because you *can* make a change. You're not destined to an unhealthy life if you choose not to be. Take some breaks, look behind you, and see how much you've conquered—it will amaze you to see what life is like on the road less travelled.

Do know that the greatest power in the world is to take possession of your mind and thoughts that make a home there. Positive or negative, you are already familiar with this principle. We see how negative, fearful thoughts can manifest into existence. This new concept is just about flipping the mental attitude to a positive alternative.

The Squeaky Wheel Gets the Oil

There's the idea that the loudest (or most noticeable) problem is the one that gets the most attention.

So let's dive into this: physical and mental fitness are equally as important to having a healthy balance. Then why is it that all the ads, commercials, programs, and facilities out there getting all the positive attention are geared mainly towards physical fitness? When is the last time you saw an upbeat commercial for someone suffering from depression? Or an infomercial on the latest greatest device guaranteed to make you "happy" and anxiety free in 30 days or your money back!

Here's my two cents … Because the media is the biggest promoter of self-image—which is mainly what physical fitness targets —that is why society has such a strong focus on changing the way your body looks. We have become so programmed to believe that we need to look a certain way, therefore the abundance of help out there is marketed around just that, changing your *body.* Now don't get me wrong, you absolutely need to have movement as part of your lifestyle, once again, I worked in the physical fitness industry and I know the incredible benefits of exercise and the importance of this routine. My point is that if you are starting or are on a physical fitness journey, the information and options out there are much more in reach and socially acceptable.

Here is where mind fitness comes into play. I want to bring to the surface the importance of a healthy mind as an equal partner to a healthy body. Let's join the two forces!

The more we can get people to speak of their mind fitness journeys and start to see the link that what we feel is what we think, and vice versa, then we know we can shift the attention society and media will give to help our movement! The only way we are going to bust through the stigma of mental health being about only illness, is to start talking about it more and also bring positive light to an optimal state of mental wellness and how to achieve it.

Your future is bright and your healing is paramount. Don't feel chained to your past or unable to speak out about your life, the highs or the lows.

LET'S START TO SQUEAK!

Mind Fitness Exercises: 48-Hour Rule & a Q

Anxiety is when we dwell or stress about a future event. When trying to live in the present moment (which is one of the most important solutions I can provide), there are two mind exercises I recommend.

48-Hour Rule

Only think about today and tomorrow. If it's not happening in the next 48 hours, don't stress about it. If you only focus on today and tomorrow you'll soon learn how to have more control over what you're thinking and not let the future imprison you. If a thought or worry comes up that is outside that timeframe, let it go and say, "I'll take care of it in a month when that event is happening." By the time the future event rolls around, you will be in a much better position to handle those thoughts of worry or fear, and they will no longer haunt you. Thinking and living so much in the future is one of the major contributors to anxiety, just as living in the past is a huge contributor to depression.

Have Your Staple Question

When a negative thought or worry arises, I have one staple question you can ask yourself.

This will trigger your mind to think about your worry logically. In turn, you'll realize how your worry has no actual threat or rationality. Let's use an example of what I would have used in the past when I was experiencing anxiety. If I was about to drive in a car with a group of people, my mind would start racing with worry thoughts like: *What if once you leave the house you have to go to the bathroom and there is nowhere to stop??* At this point I would ask myself my staple question, which is, *Why* would *I have to go to the bathroom?* It literally stops my worry thought in its tracks and I start to think rationally. *Right. If I just go to the bathroom before I get in the car, there is no reason I would need to go again. My body doesn't* need *to go more than once every couple hours.*

Using this simple question helps stop the negative thoughts and reroutes the thought direction onto the right healthy path. When we are experiencing heavy anxiety, our fight-or-flight response is turned on and our rational thought process is turned off. By asking this simple question, you are able to engage your logical brain to make sense of the scenario and bring yourself back to a state of present moment.

Mind Fitness Challenge:

Jot down your staple question and have it on a card in your wallet or saved in your phone. Limit your mind to only thinking about today and tomorrow, and then if negative thoughts enter your space, ask yourself your rational staple question. Notice how your mind and body shifts when you do this.

Awareness is key to continuing to move towards pleasure.

Chapter 10

Mind Fitness Mastery

The Six Pillars of Mind Fitness Mastery

I want to leave you with my six pillars of achieving mind fitness mastery, which I believe is really total life mastery. Master your mind, master your life. These six foundational lifestyle elements are, without a doubt, what encompasses the full holistic recovery I have experienced in my journey, and what I would guide any client through.

As with anything, small daily choices and changes will add up to big, long-terms results. Take it easy and make it simple.

Pillar 1: Brain Fuel

There is a connection between the "two brains:" our brain and our gut, known as the second brain. It's crucial to fuel our brain with the right nutrients so it can function optimally. Did you know that 90% of our happy chemical serotonin is produced in the gut?

Starting with the foundation of eating right is imperative to mental health. I recommend starting on a high-quality line of supplements to provide the fuel of essential vitamins and minerals, essential fatty acids, and cellular repair. This wouldn't have been a topic 100 years ago, but nowadays our soils are so depleted of these nutrients that we need to bridge the gap with a whole food, bioavailable supplement.

Also, I recommend taking probiotics daily to feed the "good" bacteria, which maintain strong gut flora for a healthy environment to make those super important neurotransmitters (chemical messengers that send signals throughout the body and have a significant effect on mental health).

Another supplement I would recommend is digestive enzymes. Digestive enzymes are used to break down food. Food is broken down to be used to communicate with the brain and influence emotions. It's not all about what you eat, it's about what you absorb! So getting on a good-quality digestive enzyme is a great addition to your supplement routine.

In terms of food, when possible stick to raw, organic foods. Pesticides that are sprayed on fruits and veggies break down our intestinal walls, and are a leading factor to a leaky gut. If you have leaky gut (permeability in the intestinal walls allowing small particles of food to escape), this could also be a factor in mood disorders. Nuts and nut butters, probiotic foods, kombucha for replenishing the gut with good microbiota, are all great additions to your grocery list. Eat tons of fresh fruits and veggies. Limit sugar, gluten, dairy, and meats, which are considered inflammatory foods. Inflammation is the #1 cause of "dis-ease," so reducing it from our foods is one huge step towards improvement!

WATER, WATER, WATER! Even mild dehydration (1%) can lead to mood issues, and body functions can start to wear down. For every cup of coffee (a diuretic, meaning you lose water when drinking it) you need to drink an extra one and a half cups of water on top of your ideal eight cups a day. So keep that in mind when you're yearning for that java! And sorry to tell you, but alcohol is also a huge no-no if you're trying to master your emotions. Even though it may make you feel free as a bird in the moment, the after effects on your brain and body are majorly destructive and inflammatory!

Tip: Start off with one change from the above recommendations and do it for two weeks. Then add in one more, and so on. Layer the lifestyle changes one by one, just like I mentioned about juggling the balls earlier. If you can master one thing at a time it's not as overwhelming, and you can see long-term habit changes.

Pillar 2: Movement

Being able to get the body in motion is super powerful for your mind. Motion is lotion! Often times our emotions get trapped in our body, which is why I like to say, "The issue's in the tissues." We can almost always find a direct link between what our body pain or feelings are, to what we are experiencing emotionally in our life. Energy is everything.

What's being trapped inside us emotionally will manifest itself into a physical response (pain, inflammation, "dis-ease," discomfort, etc.) Stretching, yoga, Pilates, long walks, or other exercise you enjoy, are all great ways to release the best endorphins to keep your moods on point.

Emotion = Energy + Motion (Energy in Motion). So get those emotions moving!

I'm not saying you have to join a gym or become a fitness junkie, if that's not your jam. Just move.
Go on a hike or walk the local high school track while listening to some wicked audio book on self-development. Anything. Just move.

Tip: Choose one method of movement you really enjoy and commit to doing it for five minutes every day. As you layer one of your new nutrition/fuel changes, add an extra five minutes to your movement routine. Be sure to choose something you love! Soon enough you'll work your way up to 40-60 minutes of movement and it will be a breeze! Start small to compound big results in the end.

Pillar 3: Rest and Manage Stress

Getting eight hours of sleep a night is imperative for your mind and body to have time to reset, download, and grow.

We operate on something called a circadian rhythm. This is a 24-hour cycle that flows with the sun and moon. The body systems will run from dusk to dawn, with different functions being on full alert and others being in "rest mode," at specific times throughout the day.

Our melatonin (our sleep hormone), for example, starts to secrete after sunset. When its dark/no light is present, this hormone releases to tell our brains it's time to sleep.

If we stay up all hours watching TV (light), checking our phones (light), sleeping with lights on, our melatonin doesn't secrete as it should and our bodies and minds won't have a chance to rest and repair throughout the night hours as they should.

Tip: Start your bedtime routine like a baby. One hour before you want to sleep take a hot bath, use a relaxing essential oil to calm your system, read a book, and reduce technology, just calm and ease. "Brain Dump" is great too! This is where you journal out everything in your mind before bed. Think of your mind like a computer with 100 tabs open. You want to close off all those tabs before its time to shut down.

Use emotional aromatherapy (essential oils) to help manage your stress!

I only use and recommend to my clients one specific brand that I trust because of its quality assurance and sourcing methods. You will want to do your own research to find one you trust and know is in its purest most potent form. Look where they originate from, what types of testing they undergo, and the reputation of the company.

So let's learn how to use them! There are three ways.

The first way is aromatic. Therapy through the use of smell is incredibly powerful. Nature has made it very easy for us to be balanced and well. The natural chemical compounds these different botanicals hold send different types of messages to our brain, specifically the emotional centre, which is our limbic brain. One drop of oil can service every cell in our body to give it a new message on what emotion to evoke and therefore how to act/behave.

They can also interact with our central nervous system, helping us to remain calm or experience uplifting feelings.

When we inhale them, we stimulate a natural chemical reaction in our brain. You can use a diffuser, or simply place a drop of oil in the palm of your hands, rub them together, and cup them over your nose, breathing in deeply. When it comes to mind mood management, aromatic is the fastest and easiest way to impact your emotional state.

Next there is topical application. You can apply essential oils to pulse points (behind the ears, on your wrists), to the occipital point which is a direct access to the brain (soft spot at the base of skull top of spine), or under your big toe (the reflexology point connected to the brain).

The last way to use essential oils is to take them internally. I NEVER recommend taking anything internally but Certified Pure Therapeutic Grade–CPTG. Look at the labelling of the oils for dietary recommendation, as almost all the oils you find on store shelves or online are meant for aromatic purposes only. Taking certain CPTG essential oils internally will stimulate the gut, which is our mind-intestine connection, as your gut communicates directly with your brain. For example, if you put a drop of lemon (or any citrus oil) in water, it will uplift your mood and also is a great cleanser for your body. Another powerful oil is frankincense, one of the most ancient oils of all. Known as being the King of all oils, it can pass through our blood-brain barrier (helping to bring oxygen flow to the brain), and is also referred to as one of the best supporting mind mood management oils. With over 200 chemical constituents it can perform a lot of jobs in just one single drop!

Tip: Get yourself some emotional aromatherapy oils. You can connect with me if you're looking for my brand, and start off with the aromatic, topical, and internal benefits. Journal how you feel after your first application!

Pillar 4: Reduce Toxic Load

If you remember, I mentioned before that inflammation is the leading cause to all "dis-ease." An interesting article from the UCLA Stress Lab states this: "In a new article published in the leading psychoneuroimmunology journal, *Brain, Behavior, and Immunity*, Dr. George Slavich argues that components of the immune system involved in inflammation may represent a common mechanism linking stress with several different diseases. Dr. Slavich goes on to describe the importance of better understanding these links. 'All told, inflammation is involved in at least 8 of the top 10 leading causes of death in the United States today,' writes Dr. Slavich. 'Understanding how inflammation promotes poor health, and how and when we can intervene to reduce inflammation-related disease risk, should thus be a top scientific and public priority.'"

Let's take a look at how not just food, but our environment, can be a culprit to how we end up with major toxic overload. I would define toxic load as synthetic chemicals that have harmful effects on our bodies. Our bodies need to process these toxins through our filtration organs. An overload of these chemicals can wreak major havoc and lead to serious damage. Inflammation is often times the first response, and you may see how this becomes a viscous cycle.

From the chemicals we use in our home cleaning products, our makeup, hair products, and perfumes, there's a ton of different environmental threats that are causing our body to have an inflammatory response.

Did you know the average woman puts over 500 chemicals on her body before even leaving the house in the morning?!

Let's not even talk about the chemicals in all those air fresheners, cinnamon bun smelling candles, or apple wax scented burners … yup

… all going right into your lungs and putting major stress on your poor body.

Pillar 5: Support System
It's all about your SQUAD.

Who's currently in your entourage?

Who do you go to when you need a little pick-me-up?
Who's your BFF, your rock, and your confidante(s)?

Is it your sibling, parent, counsellor, friend, cousin?

What's your Faith? Is it God, your higher self, your angels?

Maybe your support system is even music, art therapy, a solid Netflix series, diffuser blend, or a favourite tea.

Support can be a lot of things.

But it's important to know who or what you turn to that gives you relief, joy, and empowerment, and reminds you that you're not alone. Going at life by yourself is not the way we were designed to live. We are social beings meant to be amongst our tribe and other people we love.

Have you ever heard of the saying, "it takes a village"? That's because in all aspects of the meaning, we're meant to be raised by many people who are in our corner.

Tip: Write a list of people or things that are a positive influence in your life. The people you can turn to when you are feeling down or just need a gentle reminder that you're awesome. Lean on these people in the moments when you need it and let them know how much they mean to you. Go to that list of things that make you feel warm and fuzzy inside, and do them when you need a mind shift.

Pillar 6: Meaning and Purpose

To live a fulfilling life is to be able to walk out your true purpose. A lot of people don't even know what the meaning of life really is, or in other words, what their purpose is.

Why are we here?

What are our years here on Earth supposed to represent?

How are we meant to live our dash? Look at the year you were born to the hypothetical year you leave this physical Earth (for me it looks like 1983-2083). It's the dash in between those two years that matters. What are you leaving behind?

If you don't know what your purpose is yet, I encourage you to take some time in silence.

Ask God/your higher self/Universe (whoever/whatever your belief system is) for some direction.

Sometimes you need to believe with blind faith, that there truly is a purpose in this lifetime for you.

There's a gift you're meant to deliver on your life's journey.

So many people will leave this world with their song still inside them. They'll never know why they're here and will battle negative emotions and hold on to traumas instead of letting it be part of their gift.

Is that you?

True mind fitness mastery is being able to live your life with meaning, even if that's just to have faith that your current journey is taking you there.

Tip: Write down the things you do or would do even if you didn't get paid. The things that bring you so much joy you are naturally drawn to doing them. Maybe it's something you volunteer doing.

Maybe it's your hobby.

Maybe it's a natural talent you have.

Searching here you will find your purpose. Your purpose is the gift you offer this world, a way you're supposed to help heal the world by bringing peace, love, and joy.

Make a list of the things that light your soul on fire.
Do those things.
Every day.

Now that you have the six pillars to mind fitness mastery, it's time to put them in place.

Go on, be the BOSS of your emotional wellness!

The Pursuit of Purpose is Yours to
Discover...

xo,

Jennifer Bitner

Words of Encouragement from other Mind Fitness Warriors:

"It's not all perfect, there are days where I dip a little low, but now I'm a lot kinder to myself. When you look at your beliefs and dig deeper, you start to pull out the truth of who you really are. When I go through my lows, I have a different understanding of 'this too shall pass' and this isn't my life. Likely I'm just overstimulated and need time to rejuvenate. It's okay to be the way I am and it's okay to need to take time to myself. We all function differently and we to need work with that because that's what we've been given. It's not a curse, you're not a victim. It's about working with who we are and who we are is more than okay!" - Christina Tsounis, Ontario Canada.

"I used to take these words lightly, but don't give up. People look for that light at the end of the tunnel, but what I've started to realize is that light will never be there, it was never 'out there', it's always going to be within. What I love about that, is there are people around you who are going to help you reignite that light within. I started to have people come into my life who helped me with my toughest days, so be mindful about those that come into your life now, because they're there for a reason and are here to help you. I've come across so many people who say, 'I've tried reaching out to people and no one wants to listen.' To that I say, keep going." - Nadia Mastroianni, Ontario Canada.

"Be who you are. Be present and trust your most natural self. When you can just be present, you lose your worries of what's in the future or what you're holding onto from the past. Without those things, you can be where you are. The most important thing in life is how you feel, because if you feel depressed, than you're going to be living from that state and it's going to attract more things to yourself that make you depressed. It's not going to change unless you change your state. If you can get yourself to relax and be okay, and do whatever it is that helps you feel a little bit better, that's going to help you attract things that will make you feel even better." - Taylor Bosco, California USA.

"When I feel like I am taking care of my body I feel so good. We ask our bodies to do so much on a daily basis and they do everything in their power to make it happen. It is truly amazing. It is very nurturing for me when I am taking good care of myself. It is the most powerful act of self-love that I practice. I feel nurtured and empowered when I am feeding myself well, taking my supplements and supporting my mental and emotional health through meditation, personal development, exercise and the use of the most wonderful essential oils on the planet." - Lisa McBride, Ontario Canada.

"Encourage people around you and don't put them down, because you really don't know what they're going through and the smallest thing you think is a joke, might not be to them. Make sure you are open and making people around you feel comfortable and encouraged, like they really do have someone they can talk to. For me, if you could just help one person, that might be the one person who needs your help the most. Like the Golden Rule, 'treat everyone the way you want to be treated.'" - Brittany Doell, Alberta, Canada.

"Working out my mind and body daily helps with maintenance and consistency in reminding myself that, 'I can be strong and leaving the gym reminds me that I did something for me!' At the end of the day, it's something I can take pride in and it shows. The natural endorphins you get really are something that certain medications can't give you. Other than the gym, journaling helps certain truths come out of me that is different from talking about it. There's a certain level of authenticity that comes out when you're journaling. When going back and reading it, you think, 'wow. I do have good insight.' You start to realize there's this very rational part of your mental illness that knows that the thoughts you're thinking might seem crazy. Seeing my true feelings through my writing has been so eye-opening to me and who I really am as a person. My dog has also been a huge part of my life. Being able to walk with him helps me get my thoughts aligned in what is to come in the next 24 hours I'm given." - Megan Lawrence, Florida, USA.

"If you want to change, you have to have the willingness to change. We like the idea of it, but it's sometimes scary so we don't take action. I say jump in full force because it's only going to go one way. Have a team of people around you! I had a Reiki Practitioner, Homeopath and Naturopath. I had acupuncture, my hormones checked, my gut assessed, did personal development, and yoga—I did everything! You have to be around people who are going to support you and who are going to show you the way. It's going to be scary if you do it on your own. Seek everything out because it's usually a combination of things when it comes to your mental wellbeing, and don't give up if one thing doesn't work. You're continuously evolving as a person everyday, and it's normal to feel lows too throughout your life. You're a human being with all of these emotions, and they are your tool! Always ask yourself, 'why do I feel this way? What's this trying to tell me?'" - Dr. Renata Taravski, Ontario Canada.

"Don't give up, life gets better! Sometimes life gets bad, but embrace it, acknowledge it, and don't be scared to talk about it. Don't say 'I'm fine' when you're not fine. When you talk about it, it opens up the dialogue and creates better relationships. It's when we shut down and don't talk about it, the rest of our life kind of starts to shut down too. Don't be scared to talk about it, because it's never going to be as bad as you think it will be, our brain gets creative with worse case scenarios!" - Jennifer Allen, Florida USA.

"Mental illness is not the definition of you. You are not *depression,* it is just something that you are dealing with, hopefully only on occasion. If you're not dealing with it on occasion, start working with a mental health professional and on your self-care to get to that point where it is just on occasion. It doesn't define you. When I talk about my journey with depression on my podcast, it has inspired people to go see a therapist or to understand a friend better, rather than telling them to 'just snap out of it'. I really want people to know they're not defined by it, those around them aren't defined by it, and that we must come together to stop the shame, stigma and judgement around mental health. It's just as normal to seek out a mental health professional for your mental health struggles, as it is seeking out a primary care physician for your physical health struggles." - Megan Hall, Virginia, USA.

MY BIGGEST TAKEAWAYS AND HOW I AM GOING TO APPLY
THE PRINCIPLES TAUGHT IN THIS BOOK

Notes

Notes

Notes

Notes

Made in the USA
Columbia, SC
25 May 2019